GN00982857

The Path to Inner Peace

Sumitra Shakya

The Path to Inner Peace

Finding Happiness and Living Your Best Life:
44 Stories to Relieve Stress and
Stop Negative Thoughts

Copyright © 2023 Sumitra Shakya

DEDICATION

To my family
To those who are gone
To those who were always there
To those who will always be

The Path to Inner Peace

CONTENTS

The Path to Inner Peace

Begin Your Journey of Serenity

Welcome, dear reader, to the first step of your journey towards inner peace.

This book is a pathway, and each story a stepping stone to tread upon with mindfulness. Like the ancient trails winding through the Himalayas, the path before you is rich with wisdom and simple beauty, waiting to be discovered.
Just as Zen monks teach through their actions, these stories aim to offer you timeless lessons that have enlightened my existence. To accompany you more closely on this adventure, I have prepared special content for you, easily downloadable.

 By scanning this QR Code, you will gain access to a selection of free bonuses that I have personally curated: additional content that will help you integrate Zen principles and the teachings from this book into your daily life.

My hope is that these gifts will serve as a compass on your journey, as they have on mine. I invite you to take a moment to explore these growth tools and allow them to enrich your journey towards serenity.

With affection and presence,

Sumitra Shakya

 Do you like the book? Please leave an honest review, you can do so by scanning the qr code to the left

The Path to Inner Peace

Introduction

The Path Begins Here:
"The Map for Your Inner Rebirth"

In a peaceful village nestled at the foot of the mountains, there lived an old monk who spent his days in meditation and prayer. His wisdom was known throughout the land, and many people came from afar to listen to him.
One day, a weary young traveler approached him.
"Master," he said, "I am tired. I have traversed forests and mountains in search of inner peace, but each step I take seems to take me further away from my goal. How can I find the right path?"

The monk smiled gently and replied:

"Dear friend, the path begins here, within you. It is not a physical journey, but an inner journey, a map for your inner rebirth."

And so, your adventure too begins.

Dear Reader,

It is with sincere warmth and a deep sense of gratitude that I welcome you on this extraordinary journey of existence. A journey that is not just a physical or temporal path, but an eternal adventure of the soul and mind, nestled within the pages before you. This book, as you will see, is not a mere collection of words and sentences. It is a treasure map, meticulously drawn, guiding you through the intricate labyrinths of your deepest essence, your inner self.

We live in an era of endless distractions, where everything seems to happen at the speed of light. We are constantly bombarded with information, commitments, stress, and work overload. Amidst all this noise, it's easy to lose sight of what's truly important: the connection with our true nature, inner peace, serenity. It's as if we are sailors in a stormy sea, without a compass. This book aspires to be your lantern, your beacon in the darkness, your compass guiding you back to the luminous path of wisdom, mindfulness, and yes, bliss.

Each chapter you encounter reflects a phase of life, where we will have the opportunity to explore together the various facets of existence. From the practice of mindfulness to the depth of reflection, from the power of positive thinking to the acquisition of inner peace, each story is an invitation to pause, to breathe, to reflect.

Within each story lies a world of wisdom waiting to be discovered, meditated upon, and above all, assimilated deep within your being.

In the frantic dance of modern life, taking time to read and reflect can seem almost a luxury we can't afford. But I assure you, dedicating time to reading, repetition, understanding, and reflection is not at all a luxury; it's essential nourishment for the soul; it's balm for tired hearts and minds.

That's why I encourage you – before jumping to conclusions read this paragraph carefully – to read each story at least three times, and to reach the end of our journey. Repetition is the mother of recognition and will allow you to probe ever-new layers of meaning, understanding, and reflection. And to allow these pearls of wisdom to settle in your heart and mind, I recommend immersing yourself in no more than two stories a day.

By following this approach, you will allow the stories to sprout in the fertile soil of your inner self. Like seeds of wisdom, they will grow into sturdy trees of intuition and understanding. Their roots will penetrate deeply into the soil of your being, and their branches will extend towards the infinite sky of your potential.

Every story in this book contains a phrase, a concept, or a symbol, acting as an esoteric key. This key has been carefully forged to unlock the doors of deep understanding and mindfulness. When you read these stories and the reflections that accompany them, I invite you to do so with an open mind and a free heart, like an "Emptied Tea Cup." This ancient Zen symbol represents the mind free from prejudices and assumptions. Only when you are empty, can you be filled with new possibilities; and only when you are full, can you be emptied again to make room for new discoveries. This perpetual cycle of emptying and filling constitutes an infinite loop of growth, evolution, becoming ever more conscious.

Imagine now being like the "Infinite River" of mindfulness. Let your understanding flow freely, without restraint, without the mental barriers that often prevent us from seeing things as they truly are. Allow each story to envelop and transport you—like a light, delicate leaf carried by the water—towards the unexplored horizon of your true self. Allow yourself to flow, to be carried by the current of words, teachings, and lessons intrinsic in each sentence, in each paragraph.

Every story you read is a step, a footprint on the path of your inner evolution. Every reflection is a road sign, a beacon in the darkness, pointing the direction you need to go. Every word is a stone you can use to build the bridge toward a more authentic and fulfilled version of yourself.

Remember, on this journey, you are never alone. As a faithful adventure companion, I am here to walk beside you. I am here to offer advice when the path seems uncertain, to share my lantern when the path becomes dark, and to celebrate with you every milestone reached.

I realize doubts may arise along the way. You might wonder, "Is real change truly possible? Can I really find inner peace amid this chaos?" To this, I respond with another ancient Zen teaching: "When the student is ready, the teacher appears." And in this case, the "teacher" is the wisdom contained in these stories and reflections. They are the keys that will unlock the doors of your intuition and mindfulness.

Well, are you ready to take this first, crucial step toward your inner and spiritual rebirth? The path you are about to embark on has already been traced, and it lies right beneath your feet. The map for your awakening, your new beginning, is in your hands. It is a tremendous honor for me to have the opportunity to accompany you on this extraordinary journey of exploration and discovery of your true self.

Now, there is no more time to waste. The pages await to be turned, the stories to be read, the reflections to be meditated upon. Open the first page and let the wind of fate blow on the sails of your curiosity and desire for knowledge. Dive into the flow of words, let each story carry you towards new horizons, and savor the sweet melody of silence between the words.

In the quiet of this moment, in the here and now, I invite you to begin. You are in good hands. You are in good company. And above all, you are on the right path. Come on, let's do it together. Open the first page, and let's begin this magnificent adventure of the soul.

With affection and presence,

Sumitra Shakya

I
Mindfulness

The Alchemy of Presence:
Transforming Every Moment into Gold

1.
The Flower in the Storm:
The Gift of Mindfulness

In a village enclosed between mountains and woods, where cherry blossoms embraced the air and the rain painted patterns on the ground, lived Hanako, the gardener. His home was hidden behind a riot of colors and scents, a garden where each flower seemed to tell a story. Despite the frequent storms that lashed the region, his flowers not only survived but thrived in a symphony of colors and fragrances.

One autumn day, as the sky threatened rain and the leaves began to turn gold and orange, a traveler named Kaito entered the village. Hearing about Hanako's legendary garden, he decided to visit. With his hands in the mud, Hanako was gently planting a new bulb when Kaito arrived.

"I've never seen such beautiful flowers, especially in a region plagued by storms. What's your secret?" asked Kaito, his eyes shining with sincere curiosity.

Hanako paused for a moment, wiped his hands on his cotton robe, and turned to Kaito with a calm and reassuring smile. "You see, the storm is not the flower's antagonist, it's rather a stern teacher. Each raindrop beats like a drum, calling the flower to rise. Each gust of wind is like a trial, an exercise to strengthen its stem."

"Honestly, I find it hard to believe that storms can be of any benefit," Kaito replied skeptically.

"We all initially view hardships as enemies, not as teachers. But mindfulness, my dear visitor, is like these flowers. It does not shy away from life's storms — difficulties, stress, anxiety — but finds its strength in them. When we are fully present, every moment, whether of joy or suffering, becomes a teacher. And like the flower, we become stronger, more capable of facing the next storm, and the next, and the next."

Kaito remained silent for a moment, watching a drop of water slide off a chrysanthemum petal and gently fall to the ground beneath. He felt a strange sense of calm envelop him, as if he had discovered a hidden treasure amidst the storm that was his life.

"I thank fate for bringing me here, Hanako," he finally said. "You have turned this storm into a life lesson."

Hanako smiled, "It's not fate, Kaito-san. It's mindfulness, the gift that allows you to see the storm not as an obstacle but as a passage to a new understanding of yourself and the world around you."

As Kaito left the garden, a ray of sunlight peeked through the clouds, illuminating the petals of a young lotus flower in the garden's pond. Even the flower seemed aware of the moment, as if it were welcoming the sun, the rain, and the wind as the teachers they were.

And so, the story of Hanako and his garden became a legend in the village, a tale of how mindfulness can transform life's storms into opportunities for growth and inner beauty. A reminder that even in the heart of the fiercest storms, a flower can not only survive but thrive.

Reflections

What can this narrative teach us about mindfulness? How can a garden, radiant despite the storms, be a metaphor for our existence?

The story of Hanako and his wonderful garden is as enchanting as it is enlightening.

When Kaito enters the garden, he is driven by a sense of disbelief and curiosity. What if that disbelief is akin to the doubts we harbor when facing life's challenges? Challenges that, like Kaito, we are inclined to see only as obstacles, not as opportunities.

Hanako, with his serene wisdom, introduces a change in perspective: storms are not enemies to be avoided, but rather stern teachers to learn from. Mindfulness allows us to face life's difficult moments — stress, anxiety, problems — as opportunities for growth. This growth is not an act of overcoming an obstacle but a process of integration. Integrating the lesson of the "storm" makes us stronger, more resilient, and perhaps even wiser.

Have you ever stopped to think about how you react to life's storms? Like Hanako sees each drop of rain and each gust of wind as opportunities for his flowers to grow, so too might you see challenges as moments calling you to "rise."

Mindfulness is the key that transforms these experiences into vital teachings.

An even subtler lesson is the value of presence. Kaito is visibly transformed by the simple act of watching a drop of water slide from a petal. How often do we take the time to be truly present? To observe, listen, and feel our environment? It is through these moments of pure presence that we can discover a sense of peace and unity with the world around us.

It is also crucial to recognize that mindfulness is not a destination, but a journey. Note how the young lotus flower in the garden's pond seems to welcome the sun, the rain, and the wind as the teachers they are.

Being fully aware is a continuous act, a constant practice. And you, are you willing to welcome every moment as a teacher, allowing mindfulness to be your constant travel companion?

In the end, this story reminds us that mindfulness is the gift that allows us to see life not as a series of obstacles to overcome but as a path of continuous growth. A path on which every storm, every drop of rain, and every gust of wind are pieces of a larger mosaic, a picture representing our unique and personal journey toward understanding and self-acceptance.

Every storm in your life is a call to mindfulness, an invitation to grow. Will you answer this call?

2.
The Reflected Moon:
The Art of Presence

Amonk named Hideaki lived in a mountain temple perched on a hill, an enchanted place surrounded by ancient trees whose leaves rustled gently in the wind, and flowers blooming in every season, emitting a fragrance that seemed like the very breath of the earth. Next to the temple, there was a serene pond, whose waters were so calm they seemed like a perfect mirror. This pond had the gift of reflecting the moon so completely and brightly that it almost seemed as if a second celestial body was born from the water.

There was something more about Hideaki, something sensed in the way he moved through the temple, watered the golden chrysanthemums, and slowly turned the pages of sacred texts. When he spoke, his words were like the light breeze that stirred the petals of the surrounding flowers—gentle and fluid. It was said that even the koi in his pond, with their iridescent scales, swam more peacefully under his gaze.

One day, an elderly woman approached him. She was known in the village as a perpetually agitated person, always at the mercy of tumultuous emotions. "Hideaki-san, I have come here many times," she said, "and each time I feel at peace for a while, watching the pond and the reflected moon. But when I return home, the peace fades. What can I do to carry this peace with me when I am forced to return to my daily life, with all its storms?"

Hideaki gently led her to the pond and picked up a pebble. He threw it into the water, and they both watched as the ripples spread, disrupting the perfect reflection of the moon. "See," he said, "when the surface is agitated, the moon seems shattered. But it is not the moon that is shattered, it's just the surface of the water that is in turmoil."

He remained silent for a moment, allowing the elderly woman and the disturbed waters to regain calm. Slowly, the moon returned whole in the pond. "The storms of your life may swirl around you, but if you can maintain inner calm, your essence will reflect clearly, despite the external chaos. Practice the art of presence, just as this water practices the art of being calm."

The elderly woman felt as if a weight had been lifted. She thanked Hideaki and left, feeling as if she had just sipped a rare and precious tea, sweet and bitter at the same time, a tea that tasted of truth and freedom.

The story of Hideaki and the magical pond is an invitation to explore the art of presence. When we are completely in the moment, when our mind is calm and our spirit tranquil, we can reflect the beauty and complexity of life more fully. Like the water in the pond, our true essence can only reflect when we are truly present.

Reflections

What does the reflected moon on the tranquil pond symbolize? The reflected moon on the tranquil pond becomes a powerful symbol of our deepest essence, one that appears clear and unaltered when we are truly present in the moment.

But how can the story of a monk and a pond speak to the human condition, especially in a modern world full of distractions? Hideaki embodies inner quietude, a quietude that is not just the absence of noise but the fullness of presence.

Have you ever noticed how some people manage to radiate a sense of calm even in the most turbulent moments? How often do you find yourself completely present in what you are doing, instead of letting your mind wander among thoughts and worries?

The question arises naturally: is it possible to draw from such a source of calm even amidst the bustle of modern life? The elderly woman in the story represents each of us, trapped in a cycle of tumultuous emotions and stress.

Like her, we too can find moments of peace, only to discover they quickly vanish when we return to the frenetic reality of our lives. Hideaki offers a solution: inner calm can be maintained no matter how stormy life is outside. The art of presence is precisely this: maintaining a stable center, a calm surface of water on which the moon of our essence can reflect in all its brightness.

You may be wondering: what techniques can I adopt to practice this inner calm? Hideaki's action of throwing a pebble into the pond and observing how the waves disturb the reflection of the moon is a practical exercise in mindfulness.

Have you ever tried observing your thoughts as if they were waves in a pond? And if so, what did you notice? How often do you recognize your thoughts and feelings without judgment, allowing them to come and go like the waves?

Hideaki uses the moon and water as metaphors, but the message is universal. No matter what storms rage in your life, the ability to maintain a core of calm and presence is always available. The story of Hideaki invites us to investigate the quality of our presence at every moment. It's a call to recognize and welcome the reflected moon within us, that part of our essence that remains constant and unchangeable, no matter how many "waves" life sends us.

So, what is your reflected moon? How are you honoring it in your daily life? The answers to these questions might be the first step towards a life lived in depth and authenticity, a life where the reflected moon within you shines bright, clear, and complete.

3.
The Shattered Vase:
Letting Go with Mindfulness

In a silent monastery hidden among snow-covered mountains, lived Jiro, an elderly monk. The place exuded an aura of quietude and reflection, perfect for introspection and meditation. Jiro was a man of few words but great wisdom, known for his gift in helping others find inner peace.

One autumn afternoon, a young monk named Hiroshi was dusting one of the meditation halls. There, a fragile and magnificent porcelain vase adorned a niche in the corner of the room. The vase was a treasure of the monastery, a gift from an emperor many centuries ago, and its presence felt almost sacred.

Disturbed by an unexpected noise from outside, Hiroshi glanced away for just a moment, enough to break his concentration. The cloth he was using brushed against the vase, sending it crashing to the floor. A tremor of horror ran through him. Pieces of history and spirituality were now reduced to a mosaic of fragments scattered on the floor.

Jiro, who had observed the incident from the doorway, walked slowly towards Hiroshi. "The vase has never been more beautiful than it is now," he said gently, his penetrating gaze pointing towards the fragments on the floor.

"But master, how can it be? I have destroyed something precious," Hiroshi stammered, guilt clearly painted on his young face.

Jiro looked at him with a peaceful expression. "In its wholeness, the vase was certainly a wonder to behold. But look at these fragments; each holds its own beauty, a unique story. In its current state, the vase offers us an important lesson: the lesson of letting go."

As he spoke, Jiro picked up some fragments of the vase and observed them with admiration. "See, these broken pieces can still be used to create something new and beautiful. Letting go does not mean discarding but opening the door to new possibilities. And in our spiritual practice, it's equally true. Sometimes, we must let go of old beliefs and attachments to grow and find freedom."

"I understand, master. In my mistake, there lies a lesson of wisdom," Hiroshi nodded, feeling the weight of his error lift like snow at the first breath of spring wind.

Jiro smiled, "And so, Hiroshi, you too become a piece of this vase. A fragment contributing to its ongoing story, a tangible sign of its eternal beauty and teaching."

The story of Jiro and the shattered vase teaches us that mindfulnes is like this new picture: it's the art of seeing beauty even in disorder, the wisdom of letting go of what can no longer be, to make room for what can become. In the art of letting go, in seeing new forms even in the breakage, we can discover unexplored paths leading to freedom and inner serenity.

Reflections

We live in a frantic world that rarely affords us the luxury of pausing to reflect. Have you ever thought about how many "vases" you have in your life? How many things, people, or ideas you are attached to, as if they define who you really are? And how difficult is it for you to let go, especially when the object of your attachment breaks or changes?

The story of the shattered vase shows us that everything is temporary and that every end is also a new beginning. Consider for a moment the obsession with perfection. We live in an era where perfection is the goal, but is that really how you want to live? Perfection might be like an intact vase: beautiful but static, incapable of evolving.

Every fragment of the broken vase carries a story, a piece of wisdom. In a world that rewards uniqueness, it might seem strange to think that your true beauty lies in your fragments, in your "mistakes." But isn't it true that you learn more from your moments of failure than from moments of success?

Letting go is often seen as an act of giving up, but what if it was the opposite? What if letting go was a way to open new possibilities, to free up space in your "inner vase" for new experiences and opportunities?

In the story, Jiro does not condemn Hiroshi for his mistake. On the contrary, he encourages him to see the beauty in the fragments, to recognize that each piece is part of a larger story. And isn't it the same for you? Every decision you make, every mistake you commit, is a fragment that contributes to building the story of your life.

Here is an invitation to slow down and reflect on what truly matters to you. What if the "vases" you think you need are actually distractions from discovering who you truly are? What if the breaking of a "vase" was an opportunity to rediscover and rebuild yourself?

In your journey towards mindfulnes and acceptance, there is power in letting go. It's not about denying or destroying, but about accepting and creating. Letting go is an act of courage that allows you to live fully, to be present in every moment, and to embrace every fragment of your life as part of a larger and magnificent mosaic.

Are you ready to let go and discover the hidden beauty in your "fragments"? Why not take a moment today to identify a "vase" in your life that you are ready to let go of?

4.
The Glacier's Song:
Harmony in Reality

In a secluded valley among the towering peaks of the Himalayas, far from the traces of civilization, the glacier named Aruna stood as a crystal sanctuary nestled among the mountains. Its ice walls shone with an almost divine light, caressed by winds that sang ancient melodies. The snow at times accumulated and then melted, symbolizing the eternal cycle of birth, death, and renewal. Ancient trees and alpine plants framed this place like guardians of a timeless temple.

Kavi, a man in the midst of his life, driven by a restless desire for understanding, traversed rugged valleys, swollen rivers, and nearly impassable paths. After days of grueling journey, with a heart full of hope and legs weak with fatigue, he finally reached the base of the mythical Aruna. He looked up, and for a moment, his worries seemed to evaporate, absorbed by the immense glacier.

"Why can't I be like you?" exclaimed Kavi, his words almost frozen in the crisp air. "You are so calm, so solemn, while I feel like a castaway in a turbulent ocean. How can I find the peace that you embody?"

The Aruna glacier had no voice, yet the wind blowing from its peaks seemed to whisper an answer. Kavi listened carefully, initially struggling to interpret the sounds of the wind. Then he understood: "Look closely. Even I, in this apparent stillness, am changing. I am not the same thing every day. Every snowflake that settles on me, every ray of sun that brushes me, every wind that sculpts me, changes a part of me. I am not immobile; I am in constant movement and acceptance. Accepting reality means dancing with change, not resisting it."

A feeling of warmth enveloped Kavi, despite the surrounding cold. Those invisible words offered him a comfort he had never experienced. "You are right, Aruna. I have always seen only the surface of things, not the subtle and complex dance that unfolds in depth."

And as he spoke these words, Kavi noticed a detail he had missed before: a stream flowing from a part of the glacier. It was as if Aruna was crying and laughing at the same time, in a cycle of eternal regeneration.

"Valuable lesson, Aruna," said Kavi, clenching his fist as a sign of gratitude. "I now understand that accepting reality is like embracing a constantly moving river. I don't have to fight against the current, but rather become part of it, harmonizing my spirit with the immutable laws of the Universe."

Kavi stayed there for an additional hour, breathing deeply the air purified by the glacier, feeling every cell of his body vibrate at a new frequency of peace and acceptance. Then, with light steps and a heart full of gratitude, he began the long journey back, carrying with him a newfound harmony, a silent but invaluable gift from the wise and eternal Aruna.

And so, every time life presented him with a new obstacle or challenge, Kavi thought of the Aruna glacier. And deep in his heart, the song of the glacier echoed like a constant hymn to presence, acceptance, and the sublime beauty of the here and now.

Is it really so difficult to embrace change? How many times in our lives have we aspired to perfect stillness, to unblemished peace, like what Kavi thought he saw in the Aruna glacier? But when we got close to our "version" of the glacier, did we realize that the apparent stillness was an illusion, a mere veil hiding a perpetual ballet of transformation? Isn't change the very essence of life?

The story of Kavi and the Aruna glacier is an enchanting journey towards accepting reality. Kavi was obsessed with the idea of reaching a state of perfection, a stillness that would free him from the tumultuous waves of his inner being. Yet, in his quest for an immutable ideal, he ignored the profound truth that change is inevitable, natural, and, dare I say, beautiful. The Aruna glacier, with its apparent calm, is in fact a creature in constant evolution, influenced by every natural element that touches it.

So, what does it mean to "dance with change"? It is the ability to see circumstances, good or bad, as opportunities to grow, evolve, and become stronger. It is the art of observing without judgment, welcoming every moment as an integral part of the incessant flow of life. Why fight against the current when we can be part of it?

And you, dear friend, how often do you find yourself fighting against the flows of life instead of dancing with them? Accepting reality does not mean becoming passive or indifferent to life's changes. Rather, it means understanding that every situation, every challenge, every obstacle is actually a step on an infinite staircase towards deeper mindfulnes.

It's not an easy task, but with practice and mindfulnes, we can all learn to dance with change, just as Kavi did thanks to the wise teachings of the Aruna glacier. When we face reality with new eyes, freed from the deception of stillness, we discover that every moment is a precious piece in the mosaic of existence.

So, the next time you feel overwhelmed by the incessant flow of life, ask yourself: "What can I learn from this experience? How can I become the flow instead of resisting it?" Perhaps, just like Kavi, you will find a way to tune your spirit to the immutable laws of the Universe, discovering the sublime beauty of the here and now.

5.

The Wheel of the Cart:
Focusing on the Here and Now

In a secluded corner of Nepal, in a village wrapped in the fragrance of cherry blossoms and the melodious sound of streams, stood the workshop of Hiroshi. This elderly blacksmith was a sort of local hero. Not just for his skill in constructing the sturdiest and most balanced carts the village had ever seen, but also for an aura of serenity that surrounded him, tangible as the humidity in the air.

One day, the door of the workshop creaked open, and a young monk named Tadao entered. He was drawn not only by Hiroshi's reputation as a craftsman but also by stories of his incomprehensible calm, his inner peace. "Master Hiroshi, may I observe you as you work? I am here to learn. To learn the secret of being as calm as you," asked Tadao, his hands joined in a gesture of respect.

Hiroshi set aside his tools and gazed into Tadao's eyes. "You see, the key is to focus on the here and now. When I'm working on a wheel, all that exists for me is that wheel. Its shape, its balance, and its function. I don't think about the complete cart, how it will be used, or the roads it will travel on. I simply focus on the present moment, and in that moment, I find my peace."

Tadao felt as if a veil had been lifted from his eyes. He watched Hiroshi return to his work, as if the blacksmith and the wheel he was working on were in a silent dance, a dance that excluded everything else.

"Be like a wheel, young monk. Always turning, but remain centered on your axis, in the present moment. That is how you will find your peace," said Hiroshi, breaking his dance for a moment and bestowing upon Tadao a smile that seemed to emanate wisdom.

At that moment, a delicate cherry blossom petal flew in from the open window of the workshop and gently landed on the unfinished wheel. As if it were a divine sign, both startled in silent mindfulnes.

"Master Hiroshi, your wisdom is more precious than any jewel. How can I thank you?" asked Tadao, his heart swelling with gratitude.

Hiroshi walked over to a corner of his workshop and took a small wooden box. He opened it and pulled out a miniature of a cartwheel, the craftsmanship exquisite. "Keep this with you, young monk. May it serve as a reminder whenever the outside world becomes too noisy."

Tadao accepted the gift with a deep bow, knowing it was much more than a mere object: it was an emblem of a lesson that would accompany him for life. As he walked away from the workshop, a thought crossed his mind: "True peace is not a destination, but a way of traveling." And he knew that, from that moment on, his journey would be illuminated by Hiroshi's wisdom.

Reflections

The story of Hiroshi and Tadao is a hymn to mindfulness and the art of presence. How often do you find yourself, like Tadao, in search of that magical touch that transforms your anxiety into calm, your inner chaos into serenity? Yet, the answer often lies in simplicity, in the pure act of being present, attentive to what we are doing in the present moment.

Hiroshi, with his mastery in the art of making wheels, offers us a lesson applicable in every aspect of life. Ask yourself: am I truly present when speaking with a friend, when working, or even when I allow myself a moment of rest? Or am I more like a leaf carried away by the wind of thoughts, worries, duties, and expectations?

Here is the art of presence: a blacksmith building a wheel is completely immersed in that wheel. It is not a moment separated from an entire process but is the essence of the process itself. Imagine if every moment lived was like that wheel, perfect in its uniqueness, requiring our total attention and care. Isn't this the path to a life lived in fullness?

What does Hiroshi's gift to Tadao represent? It's not just a material symbol but a tool to bring the mind back to the here and now when it wanders. How many of us could benefit from such a "reminder" in our daily lives?

Remember, presence is the key to transforming every moment into gold, to making the ordinary something extraordinary. Peace is not a distant destination to reach but a choice available here and now, in the midst of everyday life. The fundamental question is: are you willing to make that choice, here and now? Tadao did, and his path was illuminated. And you? What is your path to presence, to calm amid the storm of life?

6.
The Solitary Cloud:
Observation without Judgment

In a secluded valley, a true jewel of nature nestled between high mountains and lush meadows, stood an ancient temple where a monk named Akio lived. The place was a spiritual retreat, a sanctuary for the soul where time seemed to have stopped. Akio, with his face marked by the folds of age but illuminated by an eternal smile, was the embodiment of peace and serenity. His days began and ended with meditation, and in between, he tended to the temple and maintained the Zen gardens surrounding it.

Despite his apparent tranquility, there was a dilemma that occasionally disturbed the calm surface of his mind. It was like a dark cloud in an otherwise clear sky, an unresolved issue waiting for the rain of understanding to dissipate.

One day, a pilgrim named Yumi made his way through the valley. With light but determined steps, he reached the temple, drawn by the reputation of Akio's wisdom. "Greetings, venerable monk. I have been told that you are a man of great wisdom and understanding. I have a question that plagues me, and I wondered if you could help me find its answer."

"You are welcome, pilgrim," said Akio, his face radiant like the sun filtering through the clouds. "Ask, and I shall see how I can assist you."

Yumi raised his arm and pointed to the blue sky. "Look up," he said. "Do you see that solitary cloud up there, seemingly wandering aimlessly? Why is it so? Why is it alone? Why doesn't it join the other clouds and form a storm, or dissolve into the great nothingness of the sky?"

Akio followed Yumi's finger and observed the cloud carefully. Time seemed to slow as his grey irises scrutinized the wispy white. After a long moment of silence, in which he seemed to weigh his words carefully, Akio spoke:

"That cloud is neither alone nor isolated. It is simply at a point in its journey where it appears separate from the others. But the truth is, it does not judge itself for being alone, nor aspires to become a storm or dissolve. It simply exists, observing without judgment its position in the eternal cycle of life."

These words penetrated Yumi's soul like dewdrops on a flower petal. The clarity he sought poured into him, washing away the uncertainties and concerns he had carried with him. "Thank you, Akio. Your words have dispersed the clouds in my mind."

With a nod and a smile that radiated serenity, Akio watched Yumi as he walked away, continuing his journey with a light heart and an open mind, ready to accept life as it comes, without judgment, just like the solitary cloud in the sky.

Refections

How can you live your life more fully if you are chained by the constant need to judge yourself, others, and the situations you encounter? The story of Akio and Yumi invites you to reflect on one of the pillars of Zen wisdom: observation without judgment.

Monk Akio represents that core of inner calm you aspire to. However, this calm is not the absence of conflict or dilemma. Even Akio has his "solitary cloud," an unresolved issue hovering over his mind. Yumi's question about the solitary cloud is more than a mere meteorological inquiry; it's a request for a deeper understanding of the nature of existence and isolation.

Have you ever felt like that solitary cloud, separate and isolated, longing to join the "storm" of life around you or dissolve into the ether to avoid facing your loneliness? Akio's answer goes to the heart of the matter: the cloud, like you, is part of a larger cycle, and the judgment you place on yourself is often a barrier that prevents you from seeing this greater truth.

Have you ever stopped to think how much your perception of yourself and the world may be filtered through a prism of preconceived judgments? You are trained to categorize, label, evaluate. But what happens when you set aside these judgments? A world of possibilities and acceptance might open up, not just of what is external to you but also of what lies within you.

Just like the cloud in the sky, neither completely alone nor desirous of being anything other than what it is, you can find peace in accepting your position in the grand scheme of things. Akio not only answers Yumi's question but also offers you a model on how to approach your internal dilemmas. How might you apply the concept of "observation without judgment" in your daily life?

Imagine how liberating it would be to be able to observe your thoughts, feelings, and actions with a sense of compassionate detachment, without the weight of judgment. The story ends with Yumi continuing his journey, light-hearted and open-minded, having learned to accept life as it comes, without judgment. This is a lesson you too might carry with you on your personal journey. It's not just about finding answers but about learning to live the questions. Thus, in the midst of your tumultuous life, you might discover, like Akio and Yumi, that the key to inner peace and understanding lies in observing without judgment the world around you.

7.
The Emptied Tea Cup:
Being Open to Experience

T he delicate aroma of autumn tea permeated the air of the Zen garden, where the Master, in a mauve silk robe, was absorbed in the tea ceremony. It was a ritual that brought him a strange kind of tranquility, a sacred moment all to himself. The golden petals of chrysanthemums and the small polished stones seemed to participate in his quiet meditation.

With a rustle of fabric and palpable energy, a young disciple, Taro, burst into the sacred enclosure. His eyes were clouds of frustration. "Master, I have followed every step you taught me. I have meditated under the waterfall, recited the sutras, but I cannot progress in my spiritual path. I feel as if I'm walking in a maze with no exit. Why?"

The Master examined the young man for a moment. "Sit down, Taro," he said with a tone that channeled both kindness and authority. He took a second cup from the shelf of a small bamboo table and began pouring tea with a fluid and deliberate gesture. The cup filled up, but the Master did not stop pouring. The tea began to overflow, first wetting the table and then forming a small puddle on the floor.

"Master! What are you doing? The cup is already full! It can't hold any more!" exclaimed Taro, his eyes wide.

The Master gently put down the teapot and looked at Taro with penetrating eyes. "Just like this cup, you too are full of your preconceptions and judgments. How can you expect to learn something new if you don't first empty your cup?"

Understanding dawned in Taro's eyes like a lamp breaking the darkness of night. "I understand, Master. I must clear my mind to make room for new knowledge."

"Not just the mind, Taro," the Master replied, "but also the heart. Sometimes emotions imprison us as much as thoughts. Empty your emotional cup and you will find the freedom to explore without limits."

As they cleaned up the mess together, Taro's anxieties seemed to disappear with it. Then they sat down again. The Master poured another cup of tea, and this time the liquid stayed within the confines of the cup, symbolizing the new understanding that had found space in Taro's mind and heart.

Reflections

Have you ever felt that despite efforts to grow and change, you find yourself trapped in an endless cycle of stagnation?

Have you ever thought you did everything "right," followed the "rules," only to find that the spiritual or personal path you embarked on seems like an endless maze?

If you recognize yourself in these questions, the story of the Master and his young disciple Taro might resonate deeply with you.

The tea ceremony in the Zen garden represents more than a simple ritual; it is a symbol of emptiness and fullness, of openness and closure. As the Master poured tea into the already full cup, he was conveying a fundamental truth that concerns not just Taro but also you: a cup already full cannot hold anything else.

How many of us proceed through life with our "cup" – mental and emotional – already full of beliefs, fears, and judgments?

What happens, then, when we try to add new experiences and knowledge to a mind and heart already full?

The lesson here is clear: to move forward on your path, you first need to make space. You need to empty your mental cup of preconceptions and your emotional cup of fears and expectations.

But how do you empty such a full cup?

How do you find the courage to let go of what you think you know and feel, to embrace the uncertainty of what might come?

The answer, perhaps surprisingly, lies in the very moment you recognize the fullness of your cup. The act of recognition is the first step in creating space. And in the moment you create space, you become open to new possibilities. Imagine how your life could be if you could welcome each experience as a new opportunity for growth, rather than an obstacle to overcome or an enigma to solve.

What if the path to growth and enlightenment was not a maze to decipher, but a landscape to explore? And what if, instead of seeking answers, you focused on asking the right questions?

This is the profound truth that the story of the Master and Taro offers you. Empty your cup. Make space for the new, the unknown, the unpredictable. And in that space, you might discover not just answers, but also new ways of living the questions.

So, as the story concludes with the Master and Taro enjoying a cup of tea, I invite you to take a moment of pause. Take a deep breath and ask yourself: "What does my cup look like at this moment?" And more importantly, "Am I willing to empty it to be open to what life has to offer me?"

8.
The Sunbeam in the Forest:
Finding Joy in the Moment

For the Zen Master, the forest was a sacred sanctuary, a place where every tree told a story and every leaf offered a teaching. But that morning, the sky was covered by a thick blanket of grey clouds, reflecting the mood of the young disciple accompanying him.

Kenji, the disciple, was a man immersed in thought and doubt. His shoulders were hunched as if bearing the weight of the world. "Master," he began, his words heavy as stones, "how can I find happiness in a world flooded with suffering, chaos, and uncertainty?"

Before the Master could respond, the sky opened in an extraordinary gesture. A single beam of sunlight, like a blade made of pure light, sliced through the veil of clouds and rained down on the earth. And for an instant, that golden ray of light touched a small purple flower at Kenji's feet, making it shine like a gem in the underbrush.

The Zen Master smiled and said, "See this sunbeam, how it makes its way through the darkness? And that solitary flower, how it shines under its caress? Do you not believe that, in their silence, they find joy in their simple, pure existence?"

Kenji looked at the flower, its petals radiated with light, and something inside him melted. It was as if that ray of sunlight had reached and illuminated a hidden, dark corner of his heart.

"Observing without judgment and accepting the present as it is—this is the key to finding joy in every moment," continued the Master, his voice now a delicate thread of wisdom in the fresh air of the forest.

For the first time that morning, Kenji felt light, as if the sunbeam had illuminated not just the flower but also his soul. With a smile, he continued walking beside the Master, both immersed in that fragile but eternal moment of joy.

Reflections

Have you ever walked in a forest with the weight of the world on your shoulders? Have you ever felt like Kenji, plagued by anguish and doubt, desperately seeking an escape from the suffering and uncertainty that pervades your world? Perhaps you've also wondered, how can joy exist in such a chaotic world?

In the story, the Zen Master leads Kenji through a forest, which becomes a metaphor for the journey of life. Observe how the Zen Master does not despair over the darkness covering the sky, but rather waits to see what the present moment will reveal. When a single sunbeam penetrates the cloud cover and illuminates a flower at Kenji's feet, the Master seizes the opportunity to impart a vital lesson: the key to finding joy lies in observing without judgment and accepting the reality of the present moment.

How many times have you lost yourself in thoughts of "what if..." or "if only I had..."? How many times have you let the clouds of doubts and worries obscure your view, preventing you from seeing the sunbeams and flowers that exist in the here and now?

The Zen Master shows us that joy is not found in eliminating suffering or trying to control external events, but in accepting each moment for what it is. The flower does not worry about the darkness surrounding it; it simply exists, and in that moment of pure existence, it finds its joy.

But accepting the present as it is does not mean resignation or apathy. Rather, it means being open to the infinite possibilities that each moment offers. Just as a single sunbeam can transform a hidden flower in the underbrush, so too a small change in your perception can illuminate hidden and dark parts of your soul.

What if the light you seek is not outside of you, but within you? What if the joy that seems so elusive is actually within reach, waiting only for you to notice it? What if all it takes to illuminate your entire world is to be fully present, here and now?

Reflect on this as you continue your journey, for you, like Kenji, can find joy in the fragile but eternal present moment. And it is in these moments that we realize that suffering and joy are not two separate extremes, but parts of the same, infinite cycle of life. And in that mindfulnes, you can find a peace that transcends any external circumstance, a light that shines regardless of the clouds that may surround it.

9.

The Endless River:
Mindfulness as a Continuous Flow

In an isolated valley, where the fog intertwined with the trees like threads of an ancient tapestry, grew a young bamboo. Beside it flowed a river, the Eternal River, a stream of water said to be as ancient as time itself. Tales and legends circulated about this river; some whispered that it held the key to immortality, others that it was a passage to unknown worlds.

The bamboo was fascinated by this enigmatic river and its unfathomable mysteries. One night, under a full moon that illuminated the valley with ethereal light, the bamboo heard a voice. "Why do you watch me so intently, young bamboo?" asked the Eternal River, its voice akin to an ancestral chant.

The bamboo trembled, both with surprise and emotion. "Oh, Great River, I am captivated by your ceaseless flow. How do you manage to always be in motion, never losing yourself or hesitating?"

The river slowed its current as if in meditation. "You see, bamboo, I do not exist only in this reality. I flow through worlds and dimensions that you cannot even imagine. My secret is to accept change as the weave of my very being. Every obstacle, every new dimension, becomes part of my eternal flow."

The bamboo was left speechless. It then realized that its existence was not limited to that isolated valley. Its fibers could be transformed into hundreds of things: a fishing rod for an elderly fisherman, a flute for a young musician, or even a brush for a calligraphy master. Like the river, it too had the potential to exist in multiple forms and purposes, if only it was willing to embrace change.

"I am indebted to you, Eternal River," said the bamboo. "You have shown me that strength comes not from resistance, but from adaptability, from being able to flow through life as you flow through eternity."

The river shimmered in the moonlight, and for a moment, the bamboo swore it saw faces of ancient sages reflected in its waters. "You have understood well, young bamboo. And now, who can say what mysteries and adventures await you in the continuous flow of your existence?"

From that day on, the young bamboo was no longer the same. It grew towards the sky, but now it knew that its true power lay in its unlimited potential for transformation, inspired by the mysterious and unfathomable Eternal River that flowed beside it.

Reflections

Have you ever found yourself pondering your place in the world, questioning what your true purpose is?

As you read this story, did you identify with the young bamboo, being captivated by the mysteries and infinite possibilities that life offers?

The story of the bamboo and the Eternal River is a fascinating call to the fluid nature of our existence. It's a metaphor that invites you to look beyond the apparent limitations of your everyday life and explore the multiple dimensions of being.

Have you ever reflected on how much change and movement are intrinsic to your life?

Like the Eternal River, you too flow through various stages, challenges, and opportunities. Sometimes, you might feel as if you are stuck, limited by circumstances beyond your control.

But how often do you stop to consider that every obstacle is a piece in the mosaic of your life, and that embracing change is an integral part of your journey?

Have you ever wondered what you could become if you accepted change as the weave of your being, just like the Eternal River? The bamboo, once it revealed the river's secret, understands that its strength does not come from resistance, but from adaptability. If you could apply this lesson to your life, what new horizons might you explore? Perhaps, like the bamboo, you might discover that your value is not fixed, but rather an infinite potential of possibilities.

Now, envision this exercise: imagine your existence as a river in continuous motion. See the obstacles as stones and branches that divert your course. Instead of stopping, flow around them. Recognize that each deviation, each choice, each experience are parts of you, tiles composing your eternal flow. How do you feel now? Lighter? More open to the opportunities that await you along the course?

So, what step will you take today to embrace the fluidity of your being? Remember, life is a continuous flow of experiences, an eternal dance between form and void, an unbroken cycle of growth and transformation. Like the young bamboo beside the Eternal River, you too have the power to be extraordinarily adaptable, welcoming the unstoppable flow of life with openness and wonder.

Observe the world around you now. Can you see your problems, joys, and dreams as parts of your personal flow? Have you understood, like the bamboo, that your strength lies in your ability to flow through life? And now, who can say what mysteries and adventures await you in the continuous flow of your existence?

Now that you've had a taste of the philosophy of the bamboo and the Eternal River, the next step is all in your hands. Be like the bamboo: flexible, resilient, and always ready to embrace the new. Be like the river: constant in your flowing, tireless in your quest. The universe is a field of infinite possibilities, and you are the sower of your dreams. Take a moment to breathe, feel, and be. Then, with an open heart and free mind, start writing the next chapter of your existence. The journey has just begun, and the path ahead of you is abundant with opportunities and wonders.

10.
The Stone on the Path:
Obstacles as Opportunities

In the cold and isolated valleys of Mount Serenity, a young monk named Dogen walked a path beaten only by wildlife and the few seekers of wisdom who dared to venture so high. It was an early spring day, and the sun's rays danced through the tree branches, creating a mosaic of light and shadows on the ground. Dogen was lost in his thoughts, reflecting on his master's teachings about the art of presence.

Without warning, his right foot stumbled upon a large stone hidden by a carpet of dry leaves. With a muffled cry, he lost his balance and fell to the ground, creating a cloud of dust and debris around him. As he rose, shaking his hands to remove the earth from his saffron robe, a wave of frustration overtook him. "Why must this stone be right here?" he thought.

The next moment, another idea crossed his mind: "I can move this stone and prevent future falls. It could be an act of kindness for future travelers." But as he was about to do so, he stopped. "Wait," he thought, "this stone has been an obstacle for me, but it has also been a teacher. It reminded me of the need to be present, to watch where I place my feet. Moreover, it gave me the opportunity to exercise my patience and self-control."

His mind opened like a flower in the morning. "I will leave this stone where it is. Not as an obstacle, but as a gift. A gift that can teach others the same lessons I learned today. Each person who stumbles upon it will have a new opportunity for growth, a moment in which they can choose how to face life's obstacles."

Dogen walked away, his heart light and mind serene, aware that the stone would continue to be a silent but powerful teacher for anyone who would walk that path in the future.

He did not know that, in the years to come, that stone would become a kind of relic, told in the stories and songs of the monks of Mount Serenity, a perennial symbol of how obstacles can transform into opportunities for growth and inner understanding.

Within each of us lies a similar path, flanked by countless 'stones'. Some are small and easily overcome, others seem insurmountable. But as Dogen teaches us, our reaction to these obstacles determines their true meaning. We can choose to see them as mere hindrances on our path, or as opportunities to elevate our understanding and enhance our resilience. The decision, as always, is in our hands.

Refections

The story of the young monk Dogen and his enlightening interaction with a simple stone on the path of life. What does this story suggest to you? Observe your inner journey and ask yourself: how many 'stones' have you encountered along the way? Are they obstacles that stop you in your tracks, or do you see them as opportunities to learn, grow, and transform?

In your everyday life, you stumble upon 'stones' in the form of personal challenges, conflicts, work problems, or relationship difficulties. So, what do you do? Do you remove them, bypass them, or use them as opportunities to become more present, more patient, more aware?

Think about the moment Dogen is about to move the stone. In that brief instant, something changes in his way of seeing. It's no longer about removing an obstacle from his path, but understanding the lesson that particular obstacle has to offer.

And you? How often have you stopped to consider that your obstacle could be a teacher?

In Zen thought, the emphasis is always on the present moment. Every single moment is a crossroads of infinite possibilities. When Dogen decides to leave the stone where it is, he's practicing the art of acceptance, of letting go. He establishes a relationship with the stone, sees beyond its rough surface, and recognizes the potential wisdom it can offer.

And us? How much wisdom do we overlook in the frenzy of our daily lives?

Dogen leaves the stone on the path as a gift for future travelers. Here's another layer of understanding: the mindfulnes that his experience could serve others. What if, in the face of your obstacles, you considered not only what they can teach you but also how your interaction with them could benefit others?

The stone becomes a relic, a symbol of the hidden opportunities in every obstacle. This story is not just an external journey but primarily an internal journey that each of us can undertake. Every stone on your path is an opportunity. An opportunity to stop, reflect, grow. An opportunity to transform the way you see the world, to change your reaction in the face of life's difficulties.

So, as you continue to walk on the path of your existence, I invite you to see every stone not just as a mere obstacle, but as a challenge to embrace, a mystery to explore, a teacher to listen to. The choice, as always, is yours. Choose wisely, and perhaps one day you too will become a stone of wisdom on someone else's path.

11.
The Waveless Lake:
The Depth of Mindfulness

Hidden among majestic peaks and lush forests was a mountain lake with waters so clear they seemed suspended in time. On its shore lived Master Kaito, an elderly Zen master whose face was etched with the wrinkles of time and hints of an eternal smile. In his hands, the wrinkles seemed to channel ancient wisdom, like the water paths at the bottom of the lake.

One autumn day, as the sun gave its last greetings to the world, tinting the sky pink and orange, a young disciple named Haru arrived from afar. He had traversed deep valleys and rugged mountain ridges, guided by the desire to find answers to the torments of his soul.

"Come, Haru," Master Kaito welcomed him, his voice deep like an echo lost among the mountains. They walked together to the lake, the ground covered in crunchy autumn leaves beneath their feet.

"Observe the water and tell me, what do you see?" asked Master Kaito, pointing a gnarled finger toward the vast expanse of liquid before them.

"I see a lake of tranquil water, without waves or ripples," replied Haru, mesmerized by the glassy surface.

With a slight smile, the master continued: "This lake is a perfect emblem of pure mindfulnes: deep and unchanging. When your mind is clear, you not only see the surface but also what lies in the depths. Just as beneath this calm surface there is a whole world: smooth stones, dancing fish, algae fluttering like living watercolors."

Haru listened, captivated.

Master Kaito went on: "In the frenzy of everyday life, we are often like leaves floating on the water, pushed here and there by currents of thoughts, emotions, and circumstances. But beneath that agitated surface, beneath those tossed leaves, there is an abyss of calm and mindfulnes."

The master paused, looking directly into Haru's eyes.

"Remember, young Haru, every time life presents you with turbulence, you can always retreat into this inner depth. It's not an escape, but a refuge. It's an inexhaustible source of wisdom, love, and serenity."

Haru nodded, his heart overflowing with gratitude as his eyes moistened slightly. He felt as if a heavy stone had been lifted from his chest, leaving room for a feeling of lightness and freedom.

From that moment on, Haru committed himself to exploring that inner depth, learning the art of diving beneath the turbulent and stormy surface of his thoughts.

Reflections

Have you ever found yourself submerged in a sea of thoughts, so caught in the whirlpool of your emotions that you forget there's a place of quiet within you?

What if I told you that, just like Haru, you too have access to an inner lake, a clear and deep water that can offer you refuge in moments of chaos?

The story of Master Kaito and his mountain lake is a powerful metaphor for the deep mindfulnes residing in each of us. Have you ever wondered why, amidst life's storm, some people manage to maintain an apparently unfathomable calm? The answer lies in that depth. It's not about apathy or disconnection, but an awakened state of presence that allows seeing beyond the superficial tumult.

Yet, reaching this mindfulnes is not a journey to be made in one day. Like Haru, you might need to traverse "deep valleys and rugged mountain ridges" to find your inner Master Kaito.

Have you ever considered that life's challenges might actually be preparing you for this deep discovery?

Sometimes obstacles are there to push us to seek new paths, paths that lead directly to the answers we seek.

It's a surprisingly simple concept but requires practice: how can you expect to see clearly if the surface of your inner lake is always agitated? Meditation, prayer, or simply a few minutes of silence can work wonders in calming those waters.

Have you ever tried dedicating time each day to cultivating this state of calm? If not, this might be the perfect time to start.

And don't forget that this inner lake is an inexhaustible source not only of serenity but also of wisdom and love. When facing a difficult decision or a stressful situation, have you ever thought of "diving" into those deep waters for guidance? Sometimes the answers we seek are already within us, waiting only to be discovered.

As Master Kaito showed Haru, the waveless lake is a symbol not only of mindfulnes but also of a deep understanding of human nature and life itself.

So, the next time you find yourself overwhelmed by turmoil, ask yourself: why not take a moment to visit your inner lake? You might discover not just a moment of peace but also a new dimension of yourself.

II
Self-Reflection

*The Mirror of the Soul:
How to Truly Know Yourself*

12.
The Forest and the Tree:
Identity and Ego

In the depths of an ancient forest, a sanctuary of age-old wisdom and the vitality of nature, lived a Zen gardener named Takashi. Each tree, each plant, each flower was an open book of lessons and contemplations.

Yet, at the heart of the forest stood a tree that was a marvel to behold: tall and majestic, with leaves of brilliant green

reflecting the sunlight like shimmering gems. It was a tree that seemed to have everything, yet was afflicted with an unfathomable restlessness.

One day, a young wanderer named Kaito, his backpack filled with questions and his heart brimming with wonder, ventured into the forest. Hearing of the gardener's wisdom, he made his way through the foliage and paths to find Takashi, engaged in his morning meditation.

"Excuse the interruption, Master," said Kaito, "but I can't help noticing the tree at the center of the forest. It's magnificent and yet seems... restless. How can such a beautiful being live in a state of turmoil?"

Takashi opened his eyes, and a playful smile touched his lips. "Ah, my friend," he replied, "you entered the forest but saw only the tree. Come with me."

Guided by Takashi, Kaito approached the tree and embraced it, feeling the roughness of its bark and the vitality of its leaves. "Now," said Takashi, "close your eyes and listen. Listen to the forest."

And so Kaito did. At first, he felt only the tree, but slowly his perception expanded, and he became aware of the entire forest around him. He heard the songs of birds, the rustling of leaves, the sound of the wind caressing every form of life. He felt, in that moment, the tree and the forest merging into a single, eternal entity.

"Do you understand now?" said Takashi, breaking the silence. "This tree is extraordinary, but its beauty is amplified by the presence of the forest. It suffers because it has forgotten that it is part of something bigger, something eternal. It's like us: when we identify too much with our ego, we feel separated, but when we recognize our connection to the whole, we find deep peace."

Kaito opened his eyes, his heart overflowing with gratitude and his mind opened to a new understanding. "Thank you, Master," he said, "for showing me not just the tree, but the forest as well."

"It was my pleasure, young Kaito," replied Takashi. "Remember, the forest and the tree are one. And you, like all of us, are part of this magnificent dance of life."

Reflections

Have you ever felt like the tree at the center of the forest: beautiful and majestic to the world's eyes, yet inwardly afflicted by an unfathomable restlessness?

Have you ever suffered from a sense of isolation, despite the apparent blessings of life?

The story of Takashi and Kaito might be your story, a symbolic representation of an inner journey we all face.

How often have you lost yourself in the search for yourself, focusing on a single aspect of your life, neglecting the bigger picture?

Do you identify so much with your role, your aspirations, your achievements, or your failures, that you forget you are part of a larger picture?

Takashi, the Zen gardener, gently reminds us that excessive identification with the ego can generate suffering. Your ego is like that tree: beautiful and impressive, but limited in its ability to represent the complexity and interconnectedness of your existence.

Do you ever listen to the 'forest' around you?

Have you ever tried closing your eyes to feel the life that surrounds you, the life of which you are an integral part?

When Kaito closes his eyes and listens, he begins to hear not just the tree, but the entire forest. He thus finds a new understanding that lights his path. Similarly, when you recognize that you are part of something bigger, your perspective broadens. Your problems, while still significant, find a different place, less overwhelming.

Have you ever considered the possibility that obstacles can become opportunities for growth? – see "The Stone on the Path"

The restlessness of the tree is a call to listen, an invitation to recognize one's connection with the forest, with the universe.

It's an opportunity to move from the limited identity of the ego to the unlimited identity of the Self, from a sense of separation to one of connection and unity.

And you, how do you rediscover your connection with everything?

How do you overcome the barrier between identifying with the ego and a deeper understanding of yourself?

Remember, wisdom is like a forest, and each lesson is like a tree. Some trees will be more noticeable, others will remain hidden from view until you venture deeper.

The story of Takashi and Kaito is an invitation to do just that: to venture deep into the forest of your being, recognizing and honoring each tree, but never forgetting the beauty and wisdom of the entire forest.

For, in the end, you and the forest are one, part of this magnificent dance of life.

So, are you ready to see not just the trees, but also the forest?

13.
The Deserted Island:
The True Self Emerging

In a coastal village where houses were painted in pastel colors and fishermen sang their sea songs, there lived an elderly Zen master known for his profound wisdom. He resided in a modest hut near the coast, where, it was said, the sea spoke to him.

One autumn day, as the wind carried the promise of winter, a young woman with hazel eyes, full of questions and uncertainties, arrived at the village. She had traveled through mountains and valleys, guided by stories of the master's wisdom.

"Master, I feel as though I'm drowning in confusion and uncertainty. Can you help me find myself?" her words flowed out in a stream of desperation.

The master looked at her, as if he could see beyond her skin, through her veins, and straight to her restless heart. "Follow me," he simply said.

They walked in silence along the foam-kissed shore until they reached a small boat, fragile in appearance but solidly built. The master, with skillful dexterity, steered the boat into open waters. The sky above them seemed vast and infinite, like the ocean below.

"Here is a small island, a dot of land amidst the immensity," said the master, pointing to a small piece of land emerging like a mirage on the horizon.

The boat reached the island, and the master said, "Live here for a week. You will be alone, without distractions. It's an opportunity to discover who you truly are. This island, in its simplicity, is a reflection of your inner being. Without the distractions of the outside world, you can listen to the silent voice of your true self."

A week later, the master's boat returned to dock at the island. The young woman who boarded was transformed. Her eyes were no longer clouded; they shone like stars.

"How do you feel?" asked the master.

"I feel as if I've been reborn. I discovered that my true self was hidden under a weight of fears, social expectations, and self-judgment," she said, her voice vibrant with discovery and acceptance.

The master nodded, his face framed by a peaceful smile. "Each of us has a deserted island within, a sanctuary where our true self can emerge. You don't have to travel far to find yourself; sometimes, the greatest distance is that between the head and the heart."

Back in the village, the young woman hugged the master. "Now that I have found my true self, the outside world seems a different place, as if I'm seeing it through new eyes."

"And so it is," said the master, "your inner island has gifted you a new lens through which to view the world. Your inner compass has been calibrated. Follow it, and you will never be lost."

Reflections

Have you ever felt the urge to isolate yourself from the outside world, to leave behind the complications of modern life to seek who you truly are?

If yes, the story of The Deserted Island might resonate deeply with you.

The young woman in the story is in an identity crisis, a whirlpool of confusion and conflicting emotions.

Have you ever felt this way, as if, despite all your achievements, there's a crucial element missing that you can't identify?

She feels lost and turns to the Zen master for answers. But, as often happens in Zen practices, the answer lies not in words, but in experience.

The Zen master leads her to a small island, where she is left to confront her true nature, away from the distractions and judgments of the outside world.

Have you ever retreated to a similar place, even metaphorically, to connect with yourself?

Withdrawing from the bustle of the world is an ancient practice, used for centuries as a means to discover one's true self.

And you, what would you do if left on a deserted island, with nothing but yourself and your thoughts?

How long would it take to remove the masks you wear, to free yourself from others' expectations and your own self-impositions?

And which version of yourself would emerge from this purification?

After a week on the island, the young woman returns transformed. She has rediscovered her inner compass, now precisely calibrated. She has separated from the multitude of roles, expectations, and pressures that society imposes, finding a sort of clarity that only isolation could grant her.

Have you ever experienced such liberation, such clarity, even for a brief moment? If yes, you know how precious it is.

The Zen master points out that each of us has a deserted island within, a quiet place where our true self can emerge.

And you, have you found your inner island? Is your compass calibrated to lead you towards your deepest truth?

This story invites us to consider that sometimes, the greatest adventure is not a journey in the outside world but a journey within ourselves. It can be scary, yes, but also liberating.

After all, if we don't know ourselves deeply, how can we hope to navigate the vast ocean of life?

So, with the inner compass in hand, I ask you: are you ready to discover your deserted island?

14.
The Stone and the River:
Change and Acceptance

In a village nestled in the heart of a Nepalese landscape, where cherry trees bloomed gracefully and streams meandered gently among stones, lived an elderly Zen master named Yuto. He was known not just for his wisdom, but also for his penetrating gaze that seemed to read into people's souls.

Kenji, a young pupil with restless eyes and heavy shoulders, found the courage to knock on the master's door one autumn morning. His steps were heavy, as if he bore the weight of the world.

"Master, I find myself in an emotional labyrinth. I can't find peace in life's constant change. I feel like a stone in a tumultuous river," confided Kenji, his voice cracked with anxiety.

Yuto, sensing the depth of the young man's turmoil, gently set down his cup of tea and said, "Come, Kenji. Nature has much to teach us, if only we learn to listen."

With measured steps, they walked through the cobblestone streets and flower-lined paths of the village, until they arrived at a riverbed. It was a place where water danced around the stones, creating a constantly shifting mosaic.

Yuto bent down and picked up a smooth, flat stone. He gently placed it in the water and said, "Observe, not just with your eyes, but with your heart."

Kenji watched the stone. He saw how the water adapted, flowed, and swirled around the solid mass. "Do you see how the water does not fight the stone, but embraces it in its flow? And the stone, in turn, does not try to divert the water's course, but allows itself to be caressed and shaped by it."

A glimmer of understanding crossed Kenji's face. "Yes, Master. The stone is unchanging in its essence, but the water grants it the gift of change, smoothing it, perhaps, but never diminishing it."

"Exactly," confirmed Yuto, his eyes twinkling like stars at twilight. "We must learn to be both stone and water: the stone, rooted in our true nature, and the water, willing to embrace change with openness and grace."

Then, in an almost poetic tone, Yuto continued: "When the winds of change blow, we don't build walls; we build windmills. Embrace change as the river does with every stone and fallen leaf. And in that eternal dance, you will find your harmony."

Kenji felt as if the invisible chains that bound him had been unshackled. "Thank you, Master Yuto. I now see that change is not a storm to be feared, but a wind to be ridden."

Yuto smiled, and in that smile was a lifetime of wisdom. "Remember, Kenji, every stone has a story to tell, and every wave is a lesson to learn. In the harmonious marriage of the stone's solidity and the river's fluidity, you will find the peace you so desire."

And so, with the river as a witness, Kenji found a new path to walk: a path of acceptance, flow, and inner peace.

Reflections

Have you ever felt like a stone in a tumultuous river, tossed by the waters of change and uncertainty?

How many times have you tried to resist these waters, attempting to maintain control, only to find them slipping through your fingers?

This Zen story offers us a refreshing perspective on embracing change and acceptance in our lives.

Perhaps it's time to ask yourself: Am I more like the stone or the water?

The stone represents our deepest essence, our values, and our rooted beliefs. It's the part of us that remains constant, despite the challenges and storms life brings.

But is it really beneficial to be only a stone, immobile and rigid?

On the other hand, water symbolizes change, flexibility, and adaptability. It flows freely, adapting to shapes and obstacles along its path. It's capable of embracing the stone without trying to change it, yet leaving a mark on it.

Master Yuto shows us that we don't have to choose between being a stone or being water. We can be both.

Have you ever imagined what your life would be like if you could remain true to your values while being flexible enough to adapt to the changes that inevitably come?

Che tipo di pace potresti scoprire dentro di te se accettassi di essere modellato, anche solo un po', dalle acque della vita?

What kind of peace might you discover within yourself if you accepted being shaped, even just a little, by the waters of life?

When you face a period of change, do you ever ask yourself what lesson there is to learn?

Every wave that strikes your "inner stone" is a chance for growth, an opportunity to become a more polished version of yourself.

Isn't this, after all, the harmonious marriage of the stone's solidity and the river's fluidity?

And, as Yuto suggests, we might also ask ourselves: when the wind of change blows, do I build walls or windmills?

It's up to us to decide whether to see life's uncertainties as storms to be feared or as winds to be ridden. Change is not an enemy to be confronted, but an ally inviting us to explore new horizons of our existence.

Remember, the stone and the river are not in conflict; they live in symbiosis. And in this symbiosis, both find a way of existing that is both beautiful and meaningful.

And if you reached this state of internal balance, how would it affect your existence?

How might your life flow if you allowed yourself to be both stone and water?

15.
The Sun and the Moon:
The Light and Dark of the Self

In the heart of an ancient village, where houses were built of stone and pathways meandered like ancient scars across the earth, lived Hiroshi, a Zen master whose wisdom was known to all. Even as seasons changed and the world around him transformed, Hiroshi remained like a solid rock in the midst of a raging stream. This gift of inner balance attracted many pupils, including Yumi, a young woman with eyes full of questions.

One evening, as the sun gave way to twilight and the first glimmers of the moon peeked through the sky, Yumi timidly knocked on the master's door. "Master Hiroshi, may I speak with you? I am troubled," she said, her hands nervously clasping the edge of her kimono.

"Certainly, Yumi. Please come in," Hiroshi replied with a reassuring smile, welcoming her into his simple but welcoming temple. Then, in a calm and loving tone, he said, "Tell me, what troubles your spirit?"

"Master, I find myself in a constant internal struggle. I love some parts of myself, but there are others that I detest. How can I live in peace when I feel so divided?"

Hiroshi nodded, understanding, and invited her to follow him outside, under the starry sky. "Look at the sky, Yumi. What do you see?"

"I see the sun setting and the moon rising, Master."

"Exactly," said Hiroshi. "Once, the Sun and the Moon had a conversation. The Sun was full of pride. 'Look how bright and powerful I am,' it exclaimed. 'I bring life and warmth to all I touch.' But the Moon calmly replied: 'Yet, Sun, you do not know the depth of darkness, the peace that comes with the night. The stars, which are beautiful in their own way, cannot shine in your presence.'"

Yumi listened intently, her face warmed by the tale's glow. Hiroshi continued: "Both the Sun and the Moon have their place in the grand design of the universe. The Sun brings vitality, while the Moon offers space for reflection and rest. There is no light without darkness, nor warmth without cold."

"I understand, Master. Does it mean that even the parts of me I detest have their role in my existence?"

"Exactly," said Hiroshi. "Do not judge your shadows too harshly. They are part of your complete being. Accepting oneself means not only celebrating the qualities you love but also embracing those you find difficult. When you make peace with both, you achieve balance."

"So," reflected Yumi, "the key is to embrace every part of me, just as the world embraces both the Sun and the Moon?"

Hiroshi nodded with a smile, his words measured as always. "Your being is a mosaic, Yumi. Every tile has a role in creating the complete picture. When you accept this, you find harmony."

With that revelation, Yumi felt as though a veil had been lifted from her heart. "Thank you, Master Hiroshi. I now see that peace does not come from struggle, but from acceptance."

As they walked back to the temple, the moonlight danced on their faces, and the warmth of the dying sun bade them farewell from afar. It was a sacred moment, one that reminds you that, in a world of duality, balance is not only possible but essential.

That evening, Yumi walked away with a light heart and an open mind, ready to embrace every facet of herself. And so, under the clarity of the moon and the residual warmth of the sun, Yumi began her journey towards a new understanding, one that embraced the shadows and lights of her authentic self.

Reflections

The meeting between Yumi and her master, Hiroshi, takes us on a journey of self-discovery and acceptance. It's like when the Sun and Moon coexist in the sky, each with a specific and indispensable role.

Have you ever been like Yumi, tormented by parts of yourself that seem in conflict? Have you ever wondered how you could embrace your shadows, as well as your lights? How often do you allow these shadows to obscure your inner light, limiting your growth and happiness?

I suspect these are questions you've asked yourself, perhaps more than once. Like Yumi, you too might be seeking a way to live in harmony with yourself, without feeling torn by these apparent contrasts.

The story invites us to examine our perception of light and darkness, good and evil, strength and weakness, within ourselves.

Have you ever stopped to consider that your "shadows" might actually hold value, playing a role in the larger picture of your existence?

For example, your introversion, which perhaps you see as a flaw in a world that celebrates openness and sociability, might instead gift you with a deep capacity for introspection and empathy.

Could it be that your vulnerabilities make you more human, more accessible to others, and that your strengths are complementary to your weaknesses?

Hiroshi offers a model for a balance that could be profoundly transformative. Accepting oneself means not only celebrating the parts you find desirable but also making room for those you find problematic or challenging. How can you achieve such a balance? Perhaps by starting with an mindfulnes of both, and then seeking to integrate them into a holistic rather than fragmented view of yourself.

Now, reflect: how can you apply these lessons to your daily life?

How can you embrace all parts of you, just as the world embraces both the Sun and the Moon?

How can you make this inner mosaic visible to achieve greater harmony and inner peace?

Are you ready to start this journey? A journey that will lead you to greater peace with yourself – and with others.

Remember that the path towards self-understanding and acceptance is not a journey you take alone, but one we share with others and the entire universe. Like Hiroshi and Yumi under the clarity of the moon and the residual warmth of the sun, you can find your own balance and begin a journey towards a new understanding that embraces both the shadows and lights of your authentic self.

16.
The Frozen Lake:
Overcoming Emotional Barriers

In a sheltered valley, where mountains rose like stone guardians, stood an ancient hermitage, a refuge for those in search of inner wisdom. In this serene setting lived Hiroshi, a Zen monk known for his profound introspection. Despite the hermitage offering comforting solitude, Hiroshi often felt the call of a more remote hermitage across a frozen lake.

It was a cold morning, with snow covering the land like a pristine sheet, and the lake's surface a shining disk of ice. Most people would avoid such a journey, but Hiroshi saw in that lake a symbol, a living metaphor of the emotional barriers we all carry within us.

"Today is the day," he told himself, wrapping up in a heavy shawl. He took a deep breath, filling his lungs with the crisp air, and took the first uncertain step onto the ice.

As he progressed, the slippery surface seemed to push back at every step, as if testing his resolve. "This ice is like the wall of fear and doubt we often erect," Hiroshi reflected. "And just as I fear falling now, we fear falling emotionally, facing the uncomfortable truths about ourselves."

At that moment, he felt as if the ice beneath him began to tremble. It was as if the lake had sensed his thoughts, reflecting his emotions like a mirror. With a deep breath, Hiroshi began to imagine the warmth of his breath melting the ice, and magically, the ground beneath him became less hostile, almost more welcoming.

"This is what happens when we face our fears," he thought. "When we look inside ourselves, when we are willing to melt emotional barriers with the warmth of our mindfulnes, we become capable of transforming even the environment around us."

When he finally reached the other shore, Hiroshi sat down in the silent hermitage, his breath visible in the biting cold. He felt as if he had traveled through continents of emotions, scaled the highest peaks of self-mindfulnes. In that silence, he realized that emotional barriers might be strong as ice, but like ice, they can be melted.

"It's not the physical distance I've traveled today that's significant," Hiroshi meditated, "but the inner journey. We are all capable of overcoming our barriers, of melting the emotional ice that imprisons us. All it takes is the warmth of an open heart and the light of mindfulnes."

And so, wrapped in the silence of the hermitage and the warmth of his newfound understanding, Hiroshi immersed himself in deep meditation, knowing he had crossed not just a lake but the icy landscapes of his heart.

Reflections

The story of Hiroshi and the Frozen Lake teaches us something valuable: emotional barriers are like sheets of ice we may encounter on our inner journey.

Have you ever wondered what "frozen lakes" you are avoiding in your life? Those problems or fears that seem too intimidating to face, that you prefer to circumvent rather than cross?

Here's the key: your emotional barriers, even if they seem as indestructible as ice, can actually be melted.

Have you ever felt at the mercy of your emotions, as if you were imprisoned in a rigid structure?

Like Hiroshi, you might feel enclosed by a wall of fear and doubt. This wall might appear unbreakable, but have you considered that the warmth of your mindfulnes might be enough to melt it?

In the story, Hiroshi doesn't ignore his fears; he faces them with mindfulnes. This is a brave act that we all can emulate. How? By self-observation without judgment. The next time you feel overwhelmed by emotions, whether it's anger, sadness, or anxiety, try to become aware of it. Breathe deeply and imagine each breath as a puff of warmth melting a small part of that emotional barrier.

Will it be difficult? Absolutely. But it's also incredibly liberating. Accepting and confronting your emotions allows you to transform the ground you walk on, just as Hiroshi found the ice less hostile when he faced his fears. Gradually, your "frozen lakes" will begin to melt, leaving room for new possibilities and genuine inner growth.

Hiroshi realized that his journey was not so much physical as it was spiritual. The path he traveled on that frozen lake is symbolic of the journey we all must make to overcome the emotional barriers that hold us prisoner. And it's a journey we don't have to make alone. We are accompanied by our innate capacity for mindfulnes and openness, powerful tools that enable us to face any challenge, internal or external, that life presents us.

So, what will be your "frozen lake"? Are you ready to face it with the warmth of your mindfulnes and the light of acceptance?

Like Hiroshi, you too can traverse the icy landscapes of your heart and find a new, liberating understanding of yourself.

17.
The Gardener and the Meadow:
Nurturing Inner Growth

In a Zen monastery wrapped in the wild beauty of a lush forest, away from the noises and distractions of the outside world, lived a monk named Daichi. He was a middle-aged man with a peaceful expression and eyes that seemed to have seen much but judged little. Daichi had a special role: he was the keeper of the garden, the pulsating heart of the monastery.

The garden was an enchanting place, a symphony of colors and fragrances that changed with each season. But for Daichi, it represented much more than pleasant aesthetics. Every plant, every flower, every blade of grass was a living symbol of an aspect of the spiritual journey that each monk underwent.

One morning, as the sun colored the sky in shades of pink and gold, Daichi walked into the garden, armed with a bucket of water and an old pair of shears. He began in the easternmost section, where magnificent lilies grew. As he watered them, he reflected on how each plant needed different types of care. "Similarly," he thought, "each part of me requires different attention. Some parts need love, others discipline."

Daichi moved to a large rose bush. Some roses were in full bloom, while others showed signs of disease. With a firm but gentle hand, he began to prune the sick branches. "There are times," he reflected, "when it is necessary to remove parts of us that no longer serve us. They could be old habits, toxic relationships, or limiting beliefs. Only by letting go of them can we grow and bloom the way we wish."

As the sun reached its zenith, Daichi focused on an area of the garden where young seedlings grew. They had just sprouted from the ground, and Daichi knew they would need a lot of attention in the coming days and weeks. "These young plants are like new beginnings in our lives," he thought. "They are fragile and require care and attention, but with time and the right nourishment, they can grow strong and beautiful."

Finally, as the sun began to set, painting the sky in shades of orange and purple, Daichi sat on a stone bench in the center of the garden. He looked at all he had done that day and felt a deep sense of satisfaction and peace. "This is what it means to nurture inner growth," he thought. "It's a never-ending job, requiring constant attention and love, but the fruits that come from it are invaluable."

"We are all gardeners of our souls," Daichi concluded, as he slowly returned to the monastery, leaving behind a garden that was not just a place of beauty but a tangible reflection of his inner growth. "And the act of gardening, in its simplicity and depth, is perhaps one of the purest examples of what it truly means to love oneself."

Reflections

Have you ever paused to reflect on the garden of your inner life?

Like the monk Daichi, each of us is the custodian of a unique spiritual garden, made of thoughts, emotions, habits, and relationships.

But how do we care for this sacred space? How do we make the plants of self-acceptance, change, and gratitude bloom while keeping the weeds of doubt, fear, and dissatisfaction at bay?

Imagine the lilies in Daichi's garden. Like the lilies, some areas of your life require special care, a type of attention that only you can give.

Have you ever considered which parts of you are asking for love and which require discipline?

As Daichi waters his lilies, have you thought about which aspects of yourself need to be "watered" with love, attention, or understanding to thrive?

And the roses, oh, the beautiful and sometimes thorny roses. They represent those parts of us that can be as captivating as they are difficult to handle. Some bloom in splendor, while others wither and become diseased.

What are the "roses" in your life that need pruning?

They could be old habits, toxic relationships, or negative thoughts that, once removed, can free up space for new growth.

Look now at the young seedlings in Daichi's garden. They represent new beginnings, fragile but full of potential.

What new beginnings are you nurturing in your life? What are the seeds you have planted and are waiting to sprout? They might be fragile now, but with care and attention, they can grow into something magnificent.

Daichi finds peace and satisfaction as he sits in his garden, a tangible symbol of his inner growth.

And you? When you sit in the garden of your inner life, what do you see? Do you see a harmonious landscape or areas that need more care?

Consider this as you go through your day, with the mindfulnes that you are the gardener of your soul.

Every garden requires constant work, endless attention, and unconditional love.

Are you ready to take care of your inner garden with the same dedication that Daichi cares for his?

It's a question only you can answer, an invitation to dive into the profound work of cultivating and nurturing your soul.

18.

The Mountain and the Valley: The Dual Nature of Existence

Monk Eiji climbed the mountain with the same devotion he had put into his spiritual path years before. Each upward step was like a passage through various layers of understanding. When he finally reached the summit, the thin air made every breath feel like a small triumph. He felt light, as if he had been freed from the chains of earthly reality.  Here, so close to the heavens, he could almost touch the divine essence.

He sat on a flat rock and meditated. His thoughts soared, as if floating on golden clouds. He reflected on abstract concepts like the divine connection and detachment from the material world. Here, on the pinnacle of his physical and spiritual existence, he felt as if he had reached a new level of understanding.

But the sun began to set, and with it, Eiji began his descent. He moved from snowy peaks to grassy slopes, eventually arriving in a lush valley. It was like entering another world. The air was thick and warm, pulsating with life. The sounds of birds and the rustling of leaves formed a natural symphony.

Here, Eiji meditated again. But this time, his thoughts were steeped in earthly reality. He thought of family ties, attachments, desires, and everything that gives shape and substance to everyday life. The moisture of the valley made him realize how life could be complicated and laborious, yet wonderfully real.

In the silence of his hut, Eiji lit a candle and took a moment to reflect on the two experiences. He felt as if his mind had split, as if he had inhabited two distinct worlds in one day. Why should I consider one of these experiences superior to the other? he thought.

Reflecting, he understood that both environments were facets of the same existence. He had often sought to elevate himself, to abstract from the details of earthly life. But now he realized that neglecting these earthly lessons was like amputating a part of himself. And conversely, being too absorbed in the details could prevent him from seeing the beauty of the entire landscape.

And so, Eiji developed a balanced meditation practice. Every morning, on the roof of his hut overlooking the mountain, he focused on meditations that elevated him. Every evening, in the small garden surrounding his dwelling in the valley, his reflections anchored him to the earth.

Over time, Eiji understood that true and complete self-reflection did not exclude any part of the human being. Both the mountain and the valley had asked him questions that only the entire spectrum of his experiences could answer. And in the continuous exchange between high and low, between divine and human, he found a balance that had been the ultimate goal of his long and satisfying spiritual search.

And so, sitting in his hut, a smile of complete acceptance crossed Eiji's face. He had found his truth in duality, and at that moment, he was exactly where he needed to be.

Reflections

The story of monk Eiji teaches us a crucial lesson on the path of self-reflection. In climbing the mountain and spending time in the valley, Eiji discovers two complementary aspects of existence: the aspiration towards the divine and the grounding in the earthly. Have you ever wondered why you sometimes feel caught between these two worlds, almost as if you had to choose one at the expense of the other?

In the ascent of the mountain, Eiji vivifies the concept of transcending distractions and worldly ties to touch something greater than himself. And who among us has not longed, at least once, for that spiritual altitude, where problems seem small and manageable?

Have you ever felt so detached from everything that you experienced a moment of pure internal freedom?

Eiji shows us that the aspiration to something greater is an intrinsic part of our human nature. But is that all?

Then comes the valley. Warm, humid, pulsating with life. In that valley, Eiji rediscovers himself in the context of his relationships, desires, and earthly ties. Isn't it true that the reality of everyday life has its value, in the midst of its complexities and challenges?

How can you appreciate the beauty of the bigger picture if you don't get lost, from time to time, in the details?

Eiji, reflecting on his experiences, understands that neither the mountain nor the valley are superior; they are simply different. Even you, in your journey of self-reflection, might have felt the need to elevate yourself above daily concerns.

But how often have you stopped to consider that these too are fundamental to your growth?

The key lies in balance. Eiji practices different meditations in the morning and evening, and in this equilibrium between the two worlds, he finds a kind of peace.

And you? Have you ever thought about how to balance these aspects of your existence for more complete self-reflection?

Maybe it's time to take a moment to consider how both of these worlds can coexist within you, adding depth and nuances to your understanding of yourself.

This is the universal message of Eiji's story: duality is intrinsic to our existence. Just as the mountain and valley coexist in the same landscape, so can the divine and the earthly find a place within you. Don't exclude any part of yourself in your journey towards self-understanding. And in the middle of these two extremes, you might just find the balance you desire. And once found, like Eiji, you will be exactly where you need to be.

19.
The Master and the Disciple:
Humility on the Path of Self-Discovery

In an ancient monastery perched on an inaccessible peak, where eternal snow meets the sky, lived a young monk named Yuto. This was no ordinary monastery; it was a place where winds whispered ancient truths and rocks seemed imbued with immutable wisdom. Yuto, with his saffron robe and shaven head, was a diligent student. His days were a rigorous ritual of meditation, chanting, and studying sacred texts written in gold ink on parchment sheets.

Yet, within Yuto's soul persisted a restlessness, an invisible obstacle like a thin veil that clouded his inner vision. One morning, after a particularly frustrating meditation session, he decided it was time to seek guidance from his venerable master, Master Kenzo.

Walking along the stone corridors, illuminated only by the soft light filtering through arched windows, Yuto reached the master's room. "Master Kenzo, I am investing every fiber of my being in my spiritual path, but I feel as if something is missing. Why can't I progress?" Yuto's voice trembled slightly, revealing his internal frustration.

Master Kenzo, an old man with eyes that seemed to have seen the infinite, looked at him with an indecipherable expression. "Come with me, Yuto. I have something to show you," he replied serenely.

Yuto followed the master through an intricate labyrinth of corridors to a secret courtyard where a magnificent cherry tree grew, its flowering branches creating a pink canopy. From a hidden pocket in his robe, Kenzo took out a small carved wooden box and gently opened it to reveal a single cherry seed.

"Do you see this seed, Yuto? It has within it the code to become a towering tree, a majestic being that one day may touch the sky. But to do so, it needs more than just soil and water; it needs time and patience," explained Kenzo, placing the seed in Yuto's open hand.

"You, dear pupil, are like this seed. You possess immense potential. However, growth is not an act of will, but a natural process that requires humility."

The words struck Yuto like a bolt of enlightenment. He realized that his burning ambition and anxiety to "become" were the very barriers hindering his spiritual growth. He had lived his quest as a task to complete, rather than a journey to experience.

"How then can I cultivate this humility I so need, Master?" he asked, almost whispering, as if afraid the answer might fly away with the wind.

Kenzo looked deeply into Yuto's eyes and said, "Practice the art of listening. Listen to the whispers of the wind, the water flowing in the stream, and above all, listen to the silence within you. Humility begins with the acceptance that you are not the center of the universe, but a small part of it. Open your heart and mind, and let life teach you."

From that day on, Yuto changed his approach. He meditated with an open heart and a clear mind, embraced the totality of his being, and began to see each of his failures and successes as mere steps along an infinite path of self-discovery. In the deep silence of the monastery, amid the dance of cherry petals and the echo of ancestral chants, Yuto finally found the peace and wisdom he so desired.

It wasn't a destination to reach but a path to walk, an eternal dance with himself and the universe. And all this became possible only through humility and continuous self-reflection, like a river flowing ceaselessly towards the ocean of being.

Reflections

The story of Yuto and Master Kenzo offers us a lens through which to explore the relationship between humility and self-discovery. How often have you found yourself in the labyrinth of your soul, ardently seeking a form of enlightenment, answers?

But have you ever stopped to reflect on the importance of humility in this inner journey? Humility is not just a virtue; it is a key that opens the door to deep understanding of yourself and the world around you.

Have you ever thought that your eagerness to "arrive," to "become," might be precisely what prevents you from progressing?

Yuto teaches us that spiritual and personal growth is not a task to be accomplished, nor a goal to be reached. It is a process, a continuous dance that requires your complete presence and acceptance.

How often do you catch yourself rushing towards goals, trying to complete your endless to-do list, while forgetting to listen to the silence within you?

The humility Master Kenzo speaks of is a deep listening. Not just listening to others, but listening to yourself, listening to life. This listening is a form of attentive presence, an open accord with uncertainty and the infinite complexity of being. There is so much you can learn from the art of listening.

Have you ever pondered the possibilities that could open up if, instead of speaking, you dedicated yourself to listening? If instead of seeking, you simply found?

Imagine your being as that cherry seed that Kenzo places in Yuto's hand. You have all the potential to grow, to become a majestic tree, but you need more than just "soil and water." You need humility to accept that growth is a process that unfolds in its own time and space, that cannot be forced or accelerated. You can only create the conditions, then you must let go.

And what if you saw every obstacle, every failure or success as mere steps along an infinite path of self-discovery?

Could this change of perspective be useful to you? Perhaps it's time to reconsider your priorities, your goals, and open your heart to humility.

This kind of openness allows you to accept the uninterrupted flow of life, like a river freely flowing towards the ocean of being. In this state of mind, characterized by openness and humility, not only will you find the peace and wisdom you aspired to reach, but also a deep sense of connection with yourself and the universe.

In the quiet of your being, humility and attentive presence become the silent voices guiding you towards inner truth. They are like the gentle wind whispering among the leaves of the majestic tree you are destined to become: a tree rooted in wisdom, nourished by self-discovery, and blossomed in connection with all that is. So, when you find yourself at life's crossroads, listen to that subtle whisper. It is the language of your authentic self, inviting you to let go of illusions and embrace the magnificent complexity of being, in its eternal dance of light and shadow.

20.
The Waxing Moon:
The Cycle of Self-renewal

In an ancient monastery, in a remote corner of Nepal, nestled like a precious gem among the verdant folds of a valley, lived a monk named Toshiro. He was a man of average height but of great presence; his eyes had the depth of a bottomless lake. One night, while everyone else slept, Toshiro stepped out into the monastery courtyard, his robe gently fluttering in the night breeze. He looked up at the starry sky and was mesmerized by the waxing crescent moon.

Sitting on an old cherry tree trunk, his heart began to speak. He felt he had reached a crossroads, a period of stagnation in his spiritual life. Despite being a devout practitioner of meditation and scriptures, the sense of transformation and renewal seemed as elusive as water slipping through fingers.

In the nights that followed, Toshiro returned to his solitary spot, continuing to observe the waxing moon and meditate on its changing form. Dancing leaves in the wind surrounded him as if they were complicit in his inner questioning. "If the moon can change every night, why can't I do the same?" he wondered, almost in silent dialogue with the celestial body.

One day, he decided to bring his dilemma to his wise master, Master Hiroshi, an old man with a white beard and eyes that seemed to know the secrets of the universe.

"Master, every night I watch the moon and see how it changes, how it grows. I've realized that, like it, I too should be able to renew myself. Yet, I feel like a lake where the water has stagnated," Toshiro confided in a soft voice.

Master Hiroshi, listening with an affectionate smile and benevolent eyes, replied, "Ah, the moon is indeed an excellent teacher. But have you wondered why the moon changes shape? Have you ever asked yourself what force guides it in this unceasing cycle?"

Caught off guard, Toshiro appeared perplexed. "I believe it's the natural progression of its cycle," he finally said.

"Exactly," nodded Hiroshi. "And like the moon, you too have a natural cycle of growth and renewal. But sometimes we resist this cycle. Like a river that freezes in winter, we cling to old forms, old ways of thinking, and thus hinder our renewal."

Toshiro absorbed every word, like a sponge soaking up the ocean's water. The Master's words seemed to have opened a door in his heart.

"How can I align myself with my natural cycle of growth, Master?" he asked with a tone of humility and openness.

Master Hiroshi approached, placed his hand on Toshiro's shoulder, and said, "The first step is acceptance, my dear. Accept that each phase of your being is like a season, temporary and in constant evolution. Then you must have the courage to let go of what no longer serves. This creates space for new opportunities, new ways of seeing yourself and the world."

In the days and weeks that followed, Toshiro put his Master's teachings into practice. He began to let go of old habits and ways of thinking that he felt were obstacles on his path. Every night, as he watched the moon grow, he found courage in thinking that he too was growing, transforming, renewing himself.

Over time, he began to feel a profound sense of internal renewal. Like the moon growing night after night, he found himself in a phase of expansion and growth. And so, in perfect sync with the natural cycles surrounding him, Toshiro found the key to his personal renewal. He understood that the path to deeper self-reflection is an infinite cycle, an eternal dance between light and shadow, just like the phases of the moon.

Reflections

Have you ever looked up at the sky and seen a waxing crescent moon, wondering how you could learn from its simplicity, its unchanging rhythm? Like Toshiro, we all reach moments when we feel that our spiritual or personal path is in some kind of stagnation. Perhaps you find yourself reflecting on why, despite all efforts, change seems so elusive.

But, have you ever considered that, just like the moon, you are in a constant cycle of growth and renewal?

The story of Toshiro and Master Hiroshi offers us a lens through which to examine the natural cycle of our existence. It's a cycle that involves growth, stagnation, and renewal, just like the phases of the moon.

Have you ever stopped to ask yourself what natural forces are guiding your life cycle?

It could be that, in desiring change, you are resisting a larger cycle, one that requires a harmony that goes beyond your immediate understanding.

Master Hiroshi's teaching is universal: to align yourself with your natural cycle, you must first accept the temporariness of each phase of your life. Accepting that you are in constant evolution allows you to let go of old habits and old ways of thinking that no longer serve your well-being. This, in turn, creates space for new opportunities and new ways of seeing yourself and the world.

Have you ever wondered what old habits or beliefs you might let go of today to create space for new opportunities?

Furthermore, it's not just the acceptance of the cycle that's important; it's also recognizing your personal power in facilitating or hindering this cycle.

Have you ever reflected on how your actions, or lack thereof, can influence your growth and renewal?

Like Toshiro, you might discover that the obstacles on your path are often self-imposed. These obstacles can be overcome if you are willing to observe, meditate, and most importantly, make those changes that align your life with natural cycles.

Just as Toshiro discovered, infinite wisdom can be found in the simplest things. And it's through this continuous cycle of observation, acceptance, and action that you can experience the true meaning of self-renewal.

Where do you find your "waxing moon" in everyday life? And how will it allow you to embrace the eternal cycle of self-renewal?

21.
The Empty Book: Writing Your Own Story

In a monastery nestled between high mountains and dense forests, a young monk named Haruki found himself in the midst of a personal crisis. He felt that his life was a series of actions and reactions, a script written by external forces – society's expectations, peer pressure, and the teachings of his masters.

One day, while organizing the library, Haruki discovered an empty book, without a title or words. This book struck him profoundly, like a reflection of his current state of mind, and he brought it to his master, Master Yoshida.

"Master, why is this book empty?" asked Haruki, placing the book on Yoshida's desk.

"Ah, an empty book is like a blank canvas," replied the Master, "it offers infinite possibilities. It's an invitation to write your story, rather than live according to a predefined script."

The wisdom of these words penetrated deeply into Haruki. "But how can I start writing my story, Master? I have so much to learn."

Master Yoshida smiled gently. "Self-reflection is the key. You must first know yourself, understand your fears, your desires, and your passions. Only then can you begin to write your story authentically."

In the following days, Haruki began to devote more time to meditation and self-reflection. With each session, he began to recognize the various layers of his being, from the most superficial needs to the deepest desires. Slowly, thoughts and words began to flow from him, and he started writing on the blank pages of the book.

Each filled page was like a milestone in his journey of inner growth. He realized that every choice, every action, and even every thought were brushstrokes on the canvas of his life.

A month later, Haruki returned to Master Yoshida, his book now filled with reflections, stories, and teachings he had discovered within himself.

"I see you have started to write your story," said the Master, flipping through the book. "How do you feel?"

"Renewed, Master. As if each word written was a step towards understanding and self-acceptance. I have learned that writing my story is not an act of vanity but a path towards self-reflection and personal renewal."

"Splendid," said Master Yoshida. "Remember, Haruki, the story of your life is a book in constant evolution. And the pen is in your hands."

Reflections

Have you ever felt like Haruki, trapped in a script written by external forces? A script shaped by societal expectations, peer pressures, and imposed dogmas. What would happen if, like Haruki, you discovered an empty book in the midst of your life?

An empty book is more than a stack of unused pages; it's a powerful symbol. It's a canvas on which you can paint the story of your life, but first, you must take the most important step: start writing.

Haruki's story presents us with a fundamental concept: self-reflection. It's not just an intellectual exercise but an inner journey towards self-discovery.

How can you know your passions, desires, and fears if you don't take the time to explore your inner world? Only when you begin to unravel these essential elements of your existence will you be able to pick up that metaphorical pen and start writing on the blank pages of your "book."

For Haruki, every written page was a milestone in his personal growth journey. Likewise, every step you take, every decision you make, every mistake you commit are brushstrokes on the canvas of your life. They are not to be feared but embraced. They are opportunities for self-reflection and personal renewal.

Have you ever thought about how your life could change if you started to see every obstacle or difficulty, as a blank page waiting to be written?

It's not an act of vanity, but a journey towards understanding and self-acceptance. It's a way to tap into the inner source of your being, to nourish your personal and spiritual growth.

Master Yoshida makes it clear: "The story of your life is a book in constant evolution. And the pen is in your hands."

So, what are you waiting for? The pen is already in your hands; all you have to do is start writing. And don't worry if you don't know where to start; remember that every journey, short or long, always begins with a single step. But that step can't be taken by anyone but you.

The story of Haruki is an invitation, a call to action. It's an invitation to take control of your inner narrator and become the author of your life. Every choice you make, every action you take, every thought you nurture, are words that compose the story of your existence. And like Haruki, you might discover that the pen has always been in your hands. You just need to have the courage to use it.

22.
The Deep Well:
Drawing from the Inner Source

In a remote village hidden among high mountains and lush valleys, where life flowed as slowly as a tranquil river, stood an ancient monastery where an elderly monk named Kaito lived. He was not only known for his wisdom but also for a unique habit: every day at dawn, he walked down the stone path to the monastery's well to draw water.

The young monks, full of energy and spiritual ambitions, often wondered why a man of his age and wisdom would dedicate himself to such a humble task. Why not delegate such a menial activity to the younger monks?

One day, curiosity overcame the reticence of a young monk named Yori. "Master Kaito," he asked, his voice full of respect but tinged with curiosity, "why do you insist on doing this task yourself? We would be honored to do it in your place."

Kaito's face lit up with a smile, like the sun in the morning. "Ah, Yori. Come with me to the well, and perhaps you will understand something more."

They walked together, their robes rustling softly with each step. Arriving at the well, an ancient stone structure wrapped in ivy and wildflowers, Kaito grabbed the rough rope and began to lower the bucket with a fluid, meditative motion.

"Every time I lower this bucket," he said, his eyes fixed on the dark water below them, "it's like I'm drawing from my inner source. In the water that reemerges, I find wisdom, knowledge, and peace. This well is deep, and so is our interiority. Beyond the surface, where the sunlight can barely reach, there exists an entire world to discover, an abyss of hidden possibilities."

Yori was captivated by these words, each syllable penetrating his being like dewdrops on a petal. "And how do I draw from my inner source, Master?"

Kaito placed a hand on Yori's shoulder, his gaze as calm as a still lake. "Through self-reflection. Dedicate time to yourself, immerse in the silence of your own mind, and listen to what emerges from those depths. It's a continuous process that will help you navigate both calm and turbulent waters."

Inspired by these words, Yori began to devote more time to meditation and self-reflection. He discovered hidden corners of his consciousness, small islands of empathy, and vast oceans of understanding. He realized that his inner well was an unexplored world, deeper than he had ever imagined.

Time later, Yori returned to the well with Kaito, his face illuminated by a new kind of clarity. "Master, every day I discover something new in my inner well. It's a surprising and enlightening journey."

Kaito's happiness was palpable, as warm as the sun's rays. "You see, Yori, this is just the beginning. But remember, wisdom is like the water in a river; it gains nourishment only when it flows. Don't keep what you discover to yourself; share it, and you will see how your wisdom grows."

Each word of Kaito was a drop of water – simple, yet profound. Yori understood that true wisdom not only lay in drawing from one's inner source but also in allowing that source to flow freely towards others.

And so, each dawn brought a new day of discoveries for the monks of the remote monastery, each bucket of water drawn not only from the depths of the stone well but also from the depths of their souls.

Reflections

The story of Master Kaito and the young Yori offers us an enlightening glimpse into the importance of connecting with our inner source. Kaito, with his daily routine of drawing water from the well, was not merely performing a physical task. He was, in fact, engaging in an act of self-reflection, a ritual that allowed him to dive into the depths of his essence.

And you? Have you ever identified your "inner wells" from which to draw? These might be moments that seem simple or mundane: reading a book, walking in nature, or even meditating in silence. These are the moments that allow you to set aside the distractions of the outside world and focus on what is truly important.

Kaito teaches us that every time we choose to "lower the bucket" into our inner source, we draw wisdom, knowledge, and peace. But how can you, amidst the hustle and bustle of everyday life, draw from your inner source? Have you ever given yourself the time to delve into your "well," listening attentively to what emerges from those hidden depths?

One suggestion is to dedicate time to self-reflection. This could be through meditation, journaling, or simply taking a moment of pause during the day to reflect. Such activities are not a luxury but a necessity for anyone wishing to understand themselves on a deeper level.

The story concludes with another fundamental teaching: wisdom is like the water in a river; it gains nourishment only when it flows. So, are you giving yourself the opportunity to share your wisdom with others? Or are you closing off, keeping everything to yourself?

Yori, enlightened by Kaito's wisdom, discovers that the true value of knowledge lies not only in acquiring it but also in sharing it. Don't forget that your personal growth is not just a solitary journey but a path that, when shared, can also illuminate the way for others.

Remember, your "inner well" is an inexhaustible source of wisdom and understanding. Every time you draw from it, not only do you nourish yourself, but you also have the opportunity to nourish those around you.

III
Positive Thinking

The Midnight Sun:
The Power of Positive Thinking

23.
The Cloud and the Sunbeam:
Beyond Negativity

In a village nestled within the folds of a valley, where cherry blossoms offered a sweet fragrance in the air, lived the monk Anzu, known for his serenity and wisdom. One morning, a heavy gray cloud covered the sky, like a dark drape hiding a precious canvas. Feeling an inner call, Anzu decided to retreat to a lush, green hill overlooking the monastery and the entire village. The clouds seemed almost tangible, as if they wanted to suffocate the vitality below.

With a slow, but determined step, Anzu reached the summit; the wind caressed his robes as if greeting an old friend. His wooden sandals, worn by time, were silent witnesses of the many paths he had traveled in life's journey. He stopped and beheld the view: the village was enveloped in a blanket of clouds, as if asleep under a cover of sadness.

"Many stop to gaze at these clouds and think the sun is lost," reflected Anzu, his eyes scanning the horizon as if searching for a hidden truth. "But the cloud, no matter how impenetrable it seems, is just a temporary veil. The sun is always there, behind the curtain, waiting for its moment to illuminate the world."

Saying this, Anzu gently sat on the soft grass, crossed his legs, and closed his eyes. His breathing became a flowing river of mindfulnes, as his mind untangled from the webs of unnecessary thoughts. And just then, as if the universe had listened to his silent prayer, a sunbeam pierced the cloud barrier, lighting up his face like a divine blessing.

A smile formed on Anzu's lips. He realized that negativity is like a cloud: it can obscure our view, but it does not have the power to completely darken the inner light that each of us possesses. "In the folds of darkness, the sun of our essence shines eternally. Sometimes, all it takes is a moment of mindful presence to bring it forth."

Returning to the monastery, his face radiated a brightness that could not go unnoticed. Gathered in the meditation hall, the monks listened intently as Anzu shared his epiphany. "Friends, do not let the clouds of fear, doubt, or sadness darken the light of your mindfulnes. Remember, the sun is always there, ready to shine. Sometimes, all we need to do is shift our perspective, and the sky will clear."

Anzu's message resonated in every heart like an eternal melody, leaving everyone a little lighter, a little brighter, as if the clouds within them had finally made way for the light.

Reflections

Have you ever found yourself staring at a covered sky, wondering if the sun will ever shine again? The story of Monk Anzu is a captivating metaphor for just that. It explores how positive thinking, along with mindful presence, can be a powerful lens through which to view life.

I invite you to pause and reflect: when negativity seems to suffocate your life, how do you react? Are you like the village, wrapped in a blanket of clouds, or do you find a way to reach that hill from where you can view the landscape with new eyes?

When Anzu climbs the hill, he's not merely seeking a better view; he's seeking a new perspective. Have you ever felt overwhelmed by events or thoughts to the point of losing sight of your priorities? Sometimes, all it takes is just a change in perspective. Anzu doesn't deny the existence of clouds but recognizes them as a temporary veil. Isn't this a powerful message for all of us, who sometimes get lost in the immediacy of our problems?

Anzu also reminds us of the importance of mindfulnes. He sits and breathes, freeing his mind from the unnecessary thoughts that could cloud it. It's a moment that underscores the power of the here and now. When was the last time you allowed yourself to be fully present, allowing your thoughts and emotions to flow like a river, without trying to hold back or change the current?

Anzu shows us that it's often through this state of mindful presence that we can bring forth our inner light. The story ends with a message of hope and encouragement, not just for the monks of the monastery but for anyone who reads or listens. Anzu becomes a beacon of light, illuminating others with his wisdom. And you, are you willing to become a beacon in your community? Remember, your inner light is always ready to shine, even if temporarily obscured by clouds of doubt or fear. Sometimes, all it takes is a small shift in perspective for that light to shine in all its glory.

So, dear reader, will you be like the village, waiting for the clouds to thin on their own, or will you follow Anzu's example, actively seeking a new perspective and a way to make your inner light shine?

The choice, as always, is yours.

24.
The Hidden Treasure:
Recognizing One's Inner Worth

In a particularly harsh season, when the trees had donned autumnal hues and the wind began whispering the first signs of winter, Monk Eiren decided to invite the village to the monastery for a special ceremony. He prepared the ceremonial hall with great care, arranging delicate orange blossoms and fragrant incense. At the center of the room, he placed the small golden chest he had discovered.

As the villagers arrived, they were filled with curiosity and palpable anticipation. Eiren stepped onto a small podium and recounted the story of discovering the chest full of gold in the field, emphasizing every detail such as the feeling of the earth under his fingers, the glint of gold that caught his eye, and the wonder he felt at that moment.

"This treasure," he said, slowly opening the chest to reveal a golden light that seemed to illuminate the entire room, "is a symbol. It's a reminder that every field, every heart, and every soul has a hidden treasure. A treasure that's not always in plain sight, that may require a search, a conscious discovery."

He paused, looking into the eyes of each person present as if to read their souls. "In the same way," he continued in a deeper tone, "each of you is a fertile field of possibilities. Beneath the daily worries, challenges, and moments of doubt, there's an invaluable reserve of talent, love, wisdom, and yes, even magic. You are all precious, each in your own way."

Eiren took a small gemstone from the chest for each person and handed it to them, accompanied by a smile and a nod of encouragement. "Carry this stone as a reminder," he said. "As a symbol of the treasure you have inside. And do not allow anyone, not even yourself, to forget how precious you are."

Many left the monastery that evening with tearful eyes, but full hearts. The story and ceremony became legendary in the village, but more than anything, each began to look at themselves and others with new eyes. A widespread feeling of self-recognition and mutual respect began to blossom, as if Eiren had planted a golden seed in the soul of every villager. And so, the hidden treasure in the field became a shared treasure, a precious lesson that enriched not just the life of the wise monk but an entire community.

Reflections

In this sweet and meaningful Zen story, we can glimpse many crucial elements related to your self-evaluation and self-esteem. Have you ever stopped to reflect on what treasures your "inner field" might be hiding?

Amidst the frenzy of life, responsibilities, and worries, it might be easy to forget that you exist, with all your intrinsic value. But just like the field where Monk Eiren discovered the golden chest, you too have an invaluable treasure within you. It might not be immediately visible, buried under layers of doubt, fear, or insecurity, but it's there.

In the story, Eiren distributes a precious stone to each villager as a reminder of the inner treasure that each of us possesses. Like the villagers in the story, you too possess a unique light, talent, and wisdom that are your own. What precious stone resides in your heart? And what prevents you from recognizing it?

The monk uses a ceremony to help the villagers understand how precious they are. It's a moment of pause, an interval in everyday life where people are brought to a deeper mindfulnes. Have you ever allowed yourself such space? A moment of quiet to dig deep within yourself, to recognize and honor your value? In this space, you can also make a symbolic gesture: choose an object that represents you, reminding you of how precious you are. Carry it with you, and every time you touch or see it, let it bring you back to this mindfulnes.

Eiren doesn't stop at the simple revelation of the treasure; he goes further, sharing its symbolic meaning with the entire community and enriching everyone. Have you ever thought that recognizing your value could not only improve your life but also the lives of those around you? When you shine, when you allow yourself to be authentically yourself, you become a beacon for others. Your light, which you recognize and honor, enables other people to do the same. Eiren's ceremony created a wave of self-recognition and mutual respect. Imagine the power of such recognition in your personal and professional world.

In the story, the discovery of the treasure becomes a precious lesson that enriches an entire community. What if your inner treasure had the power to do the same? What if just the act of recognizing and honoring your value could inspire others to do the same? This Zen story invites you to look beyond appearances, beyond challenges and moments of doubt, and to recognize the treasure that resides within you. Don't allow anyone, not even yourself, to forget how precious you are.

25.
The Golden Bridge:
Connecting Dreams and Reality with Positive Thinking

There was something extraordinary in the valley nestled between two lush hills, an energy sharpened by the weight of unfulfilled dreams. The inhabitants of the nearby village often stopped at its edge, contemplating the metaphorical and physical distance that separated the life they led from the life they desired. Jiro, a monk with a gray beard and eyes shining like stars, noticed this collective melancholy. Walking through the tall grass and wildflowers of the valley, he pondered the seemingly insurmountable division.

"If only there were a way to unite these two worlds," thought Jiro, his face turned to the sky as if seeking an answer in the clouds. It was at that moment that a brilliant idea crossed his mind, an idea as bold as it was simple: a bridge.

But not just any bridge, made of stone and wood. Jiro envisioned a bridge of gold, strong and luminous, resistant to the harshest weather and shining under the warmth of the sun. This vision filled him so deeply that he could almost feel its warmth under his bare feet.

Armed with this burning dream, Jiro returned to the monastery, shared his vision with his fellow monks, and began gathering the necessary materials. He chose the strongest wood for the structure and the most solid stones for the foundations. But the finishing touch would be a light coating of gold, a symbol of the power of positive thinking.

For weeks that seemed endless, Jiro worked from dawn until dusk. As he hammered, sawed, and assembled, he was not alone. His brother monks and some villagers, inspired by his unwavering dedication, joined him. But it was not just hands building the bridge; it was the energy of positive thinking that seemed to fuel every action, making the work not only possible but almost miraculous.

And finally, on a day that seemed like any other but would be remembered for generations, the bridge was completed. Its golden beams shone in the sun, creating a bright path across the valley. Jiro, standing at the center of his masterpiece, felt a wave of gratitude and fulfillment.

Soon, news of the Golden Bridge spread like wildfire in the dry forest of summer. Travelers began to converge on the site, walking with uncertain steps on the bridge, only to find themselves on the other side with expressions of pure wonder on their faces.

"See," said Jiro, gathering people around him as the sunset rays danced on the golden beams, "when we allow positive thinking to guide us, our dreams are no longer separated from our reality. They are like the ends of this bridge, now joined in a magnificent arc across life's challenges."

Jiro knew that the bridge was not just a physical construction; it was a symbol. A monument to the power of positive thinking, to the human ability to transform obstacles into opportunities, to connect what seems divided, and to shine inner light even in the darkest corners of existence.

And so, the Golden Bridge became not just a physical passage but also a spiritual path, a way for the heart and soul. An eternal testament to what is possible when we allow our thoughts to be like gold: precious, pure, and infinitely capable of connecting dreams and reality.

Reflections

How do we interpret the story "The Golden Bridge"? This Zen narrative is a journey through the potentials inherent in positive thinking, a lesson embodied by Jiro and his golden masterpiece.

I invite you to take a moment to contemplate your personal valley, the gap between the life you live and the one you desire. Has it ever seemed insurmountable to you? The valley in the story symbolizes the challenges, fears, and doubts we all face. It's that distance between "what is" and "what could be." You too have faced this space, haven't you? Yet, have you ever stopped to reflect on what a bridge connecting these two worlds might look like?

Jiro, in his wisdom, didn't build an ordinary bridge; he erected a Golden Bridge, supported by the power of positive thinking. The choice of gold is no accident. It's a precious and enduring metal, just like the positive thoughts that can be your armor against life's storms. Have you ever thought about what materials you would use to build your personal bridge?

Perhaps the most extraordinary aspect of the story is the community that comes together around Jiro. The power of positive thinking is not just a personal journey but a collective one. In the same way, your positive thoughts can not only elevate you but also inspire others to do the same. Who in your life might join you in building your Golden Bridge?

The fundamental message is clear: positive thinking is not mere superficial optimism. It's an active force, capable of transforming reality. And the realization of the bridge? It's the materialization of human potential, the embodiment of possibility. When was the last time you allowed your thoughts to be like gold: precious, pure, and capable of creating connections?

The Golden Bridge is more than a physical structure; it's a spiritual path, a bridge between the heart and the soul. So, what Golden Bridge are you waiting to build in your life? The story of Jiro invites you to pick up the hammer and nails of positive thinking and get to work. Because, in the end, it's not the bridge that carries you across the valley, but the inner strength that allows you to build it.

.

26.
The River of Hope:
Maintaining Optimism in Difficult Times

In a remote region, where mountains embraced the sky and flowers colored the meadows like silk carpets, there was a village known for its tranquility and wisdom. At the heart of this community lived Kaito, a monk whose heart was as vast as his stature.

But during that time, the village was enduring a terrible period. Torrential rains fell relentlessly from the sky, flooding fields and destroying crops. The once happy and proactive villagers now seemed defeated, their faces shadowed by despair. And even Kaito, with all his positive spirit, felt the burden of these hard times.

One morning, Kaito decided to take a walk to reflect. The river flowing beside the village, once calm and serene, had turned into a tumult of dark and turbulent waters. Standing in front of the river, Kaito saw in its flow a symbol of the challenges he and the entire community were facing.

"I am like this river," thought Kaito. "If I fall into the darkness of pessimism, how can I hope to navigate life's difficulties?"

But at that moment, an ancient teaching came to mind, like a ray of sunshine through the clouds: "The mind is everything; what you think, you become." It was a principle he had always kept close to heart, but now it seemed more relevant than ever.

Taking a deep breath, Kaito closed his eyes and began to meditate on the power of positive thinking. He imagined himself already on the other side of the river, smiling and rejuvenated, as if he had just discovered a pearl of wisdom in a shell of fate. He felt hope flow within him like an unstoppable current, radiating from the depths of his being.

Opening his eyes, Kaito saw the river in a new light. Yes, the waters were still dark and tumultuous, but now he also saw potential for change and growth. With a smile of determination, he removed his sandals and stepped into the water.

The currents were strong, almost as if nature itself was testing his resolve. But Kaito was supported by something stronger than the turbulent waters: the strength of his positive thoughts and unconditional hope. Each step he took seemed guided by an invisible force propelling him forward, overcoming the water's resistance.

Finally, after what seemed like an eternity, Kaito reached the other shore. And as he looked back at the river he had just crossed, he realized that his journey was more than a mere physical crossing; it was a journey of the mind and soul.

Back in the village, Kaito shared his experience and the wisdom he had gained with others. And strangely, though the conditions hadn't changed, something in the village seemed to transform. The inhabitants began to see their challenges not as insurmountable obstacles, but as opportunities for growth and learning.

"Maintaining optimism in difficult times is not an act of denial," Kaito told his friends and neighbors, "but an act of courage. For when we are able to see light even in darkness, then we know we have found the true power of positive thinking."

And so, even though the rains didn't stop immediately, and the village's difficulties didn't disappear in an instant, the people began to feel something they hadn't felt in a long time: HOPE.

And for Kaito, this was the greatest treasure of all, a golden bridge connecting the challenges of the present with the possibilities of the future.

Reflections

Have you ever found yourself in a situation where everything seems to go wrong, and hope is the last thing you have?

Take a moment and ask yourself: "If I fall into the darkness of pessimism, how can I hope to navigate life's difficulties?" Kaito, the protagonist, represents each of us in moments when life tests us. His village goes through a hard time, with the river, once calm, becoming a tumult of dark waters. Similarly, life can be turbulent. But like Kaito, you have the chance to stop and reflect: is it the darkness of the moment that defines you or the light of your perspective?

The power of the story lies in the ancient teaching Kaito recalls: "The mind is everything; what you think, you become." Like Kaito, you too can draw on this principle. It's easy to be brought down by the environment or circumstances, but have you considered that your mental state might be the key to overcoming obstacles?

Immersed in the murky waters, Kaito finds drive in the invisible force of positive thinking. It's a powerful reminder that, despite external resistance, your internal mindset can provide the strength to overcome. Have you ever wondered how powerful your positive thinking could be when you find yourself in turbulent waters?

Another key point is the change Kaito brings to his community. Sometimes, your way of facing challenges can inspire others to see their difficulties as opportunities. How often do you realize the impact your perspective can have on the world around you?

Kaito teaches us that maintaining optimism is not an act of denial, but an act of courage. This invites you to look beyond the apparent darkness of your problems, discovering the light of possibilities and growth. Can you find hope within you, just like Kaito?

The story concludes on a note of hope, not just for Kaito but for his entire village. Here's the beauty of positive thinking: ...it may not immediately change your circumstances, but it changes you. And when you change, the circumstances around you begin to shift imperceptibly... Have you ever stopped to think about the power of hope in your journey?

In the end, Kaito's journey is also your journey. A path that is not just physical, but spiritual and emotional. Hope is that golden bridge connecting you with the infinite possibilities of tomorrow.

27.
The Flowering Garden: Cultivating Inner Joy

The monastery of Haru, nestled among the high peaks of the mountains, was a place that exuded a sense of peace and profound reflection. It seemed that every rock, every blade of grass, every tree told a story of harmony with the universe. But what caught everyone's attention was Haru's garden, an unexpected corner of paradise, an explosion of colors and scents that seemed to defy the very nature of the surrounding environment.

Imagine a living work of art, where Haru's brush painted the petals of each flower, where every breath of wind sounded like an ethereal melody. It was an oasis of light in a world that often seemed dark. To anyone visiting the monastery, it was clear that this garden was the externalized soul of Haru.

One August morning, as the rising sun cast its first warm rays over those sacred mountains, one of the monastery's students, a young man named Tetsu, was drawn by the scent of jasmine in the air and decided to approach the master. His mind buzzed with questions, like a flower waiting to bloom.

"Master Haru," Tetsu began, his words laden with respect and almost childlike curiosity, "your garden is like a daydream. How do you create such beauty in such a hostile place?"

Haru, whose wrinkled skin seemed made of the same earth he tended, put down his wooden watering can and looked up at the young student. His eyes twinkled like stars on a clear night. "Ah, Tetsu, the answer is simpler than you might imagine. You see, every plant in this garden is like a thought in my mind. When I flood the roots with pure water, when I nourish the soil with rich, organic compounds, the plants grow strong and beautiful."

Tetsu remained silent for a moment, absorbing the wisdom emanating from Haru's words. "Are there no weeds in this miraculous garden? No unwanted plant trying to choke the others?"

Haru replied with a knowing smile. "Ah, the weeds! Yes, they exist. They are the doubts, the fears, the obstacles we encounter on the path of life. But, like an expert gardener, as soon as I see an intrusion, I recognize it for what it is and root it out. In doing so, I make room for new seeds, new opportunities, and new achievements."

Tetsu felt as if a veil had been lifted from his understanding. "So, your garden is a reflection of your mind, an extension of who you truly are."

"Exactly, my young friend," said Haru, returning to his plants. "If you cultivate the garden of your mind with the same care and attention with which you cultivate a physical garden, then you too can live in a world that is perpetually blooming. Thus, you will see that both inside and outside of you, everything will be a flowering garden."

With that revelation, Tetsu felt something change within him, as if an invisible bud had finally found the sunlight. He thanked the master and walked away, but Haru's words nestled in him like seeds in the fertile soil of his soul, ready to sprout and bloom in the garden of his future.

Reflections

Have you ever stopped to reflect on the garden of your mind? Like in a real garden, every thought is a seed with the potential to sprout and bloom. But not all seeds are equal, are they? Some bring forth radiant flowers, while others give life to unwanted weeds. How do you interact with these seeds? Do you ever find yourself nurturing negative thoughts, allowing them to choke out the more beautiful plants?

In the story of Haru and Tetsu, the flowering garden is not just an external landscape; it's also a profound metaphor for Haru's mind. Every plant, every flower represents a thought, an emotion, or an aspiration that has been carefully cultivated. Have you ever wondered how you can cultivate thoughts and emotions that bring you joy, peace, and fulfillment?

Haru teaches us a vital lesson: the way we care for our internal garden is crucial for its prosperity. As Haru waters and nourishes his plants, we must do the same with our thoughts and emotions. This goes beyond mere "positive thinking"; it's a conscious and ongoing action. Have you ever stopped to actively "weed out" negative thoughts and "plant" new positive thoughts in your mental "soil"?

But what about the weeds, those unwanted thoughts and feelings that inevitably appear? Haru shows us that recognition and timely action are key. Uprooting an unwanted plant is not just a physical action, but also an act of love towards the garden as a whole. Similarly, when we face our doubts and fears with mindfulnes, we are taking a significant step towards cultivating a healthier and happier mind. When was the last time you recognized and addressed your negative thoughts and feelings, rather than letting them grow unchecked?

Haru's final revelation is perhaps the most profound: the external world is a reflection of our internal world. If our internal garden is blooming, we will see that beauty reflected all around us. This is not just optimism, it's a path to a more conscious and centered life. So, what kind of seed will you choose to plant today in the garden of your mind? How will you nurture that seed to make it flourish and prosper? I hope you can take a moment to reflect on these questions, and perhaps discover your personal flowering garden, a place not just of aesthetic beauty, but also of deep internal wisdom.

28.
The Shooting Star:
Realizing Wishes through Positive Will

In a Zen monastery perched on a hill, surrounded by ancient and lush forests, the monks spent their days in meditation and study. The halls were filled with the scent of incense and the sound of sutra chants. But that night, one of the monks, Jiro, felt restless. There was something in the air, an almost palpable sense of power and possibility.

As his brother monks retired to their cells for the evening meditation, Jiro felt drawn to the outside garden. He passed through the carved wooden doors, his bare feet touching the cold stone path, and found himself immersed in an ocean of silence. Every plant, every tree, seemed to be in deep meditation, as if sharing a secret with the universe.

In the midst of the garden, Jiro looked up at the sky. The stars were like jewels set in the black velvet of the night. At that moment, a shooting star fell, breaking the celestial silence with a trail of sparkling light. Like a brush dipped in the ink of eternity, it drew a luminous arc across the sky.

Jiro stood still, his breath suspended, his heart open. "A sign," he thought. "An opening in the very fabric of reality." With a deep breath, he closed his eyes and made a wish. It wasn't a wish for material goods or personal success, but rather a wish that came from a place of pure love and positive will: that his monastery might become a beacon of light for lost souls, a sanctuary of wisdom and serenity.

Reopening his eyes, Jiro felt as if a new energy had infused him, as if the shooting star had left a spark of its light deep in his heart. He returned inside the monastery with a renewed determination, his face illuminated by a serene and radiant smile.

In the days and weeks that followed, the atmosphere in the monastery seemed transformed. Jiro's words during lessons became more powerful, charged with transcendent wisdom and energy. The young students listened with wide eyes and hearts, absorbing the words like fertile ground welcomes spring rain.

The monastery began to radiate a tangible energy of serenity and peace. People from all walks of life and geographical backgrounds started arriving, drawn by the growing reputation of the monastery as a beacon of wisdom. Many attributed this change to Jiro's presence and teaching, yet when asked what the secret to such success was, Jiro humbly smiled.

"I simply made a wish upon a shooting star," he would reply. "But a wish is nothing without the commitment to realize it. I worked with all my being to make it a reality, and so should anyone who has a dream in their heart."

Thus, the monastery became a beacon, not just of physical light but also of spiritual enlightenment; a refuge where people could find their way in the labyrinthine jungle of life. And all this, thanks to a shooting star and the positive will of a monk who knew that wishes, when nourished by actions and pure intentions, could indeed become reality.

Reflections

Jiro offers us a profound insight into the combined power of wishes and intentional action. How many of us have watched a shooting star in the sky and made a wish? And how many of these wishes have remained mere thoughts, destined to fade away like the shooting star itself?

But consider this: a wish without action is like a seed without fertile ground. It may have the potential to become something extraordinary, but without the right context, it will always remain an inert seed. Jiro didn't just make a wish; he worked with all his being to realize it. How can you inject such determination into your life?

Have you ever been in a place or a moment in your life where you felt all possibilities were within your reach? Jiro recognized this feeling and acted accordingly, bringing his wish to make the monastery a beacon of light for lost souls to life. This story teaches us that every wish, supported by positive will and concrete actions, has the power to transform not just our own lives, but also those of others.

What's holding you back from realizing your deepest wishes? Perhaps it's the fear of failure, or maybe you're stuck in the relentless cycle of the everyday, too buried in commitments to stop and contemplate the stars. This moment is an invitation to take a pause, to look up at the sky, and reconnect with your deepest desires.

And once you've expressed your wish, what do you do to actualize it? Beyond the romanticism of a wish made under a starry sky lies a tangible commitment required to make any wish a reality. Like Jiro, you too can transform the energy of a simple wish into a catalyzing power that changes the environment around you. Have you ever considered what small steps you might take to make your wishes come true?

In the story, Jiro's action has a ripple effect that extends well beyond the monastery, attracting people from various parts of the world. What if every one of your wishes had the power to create a similar effect, to be a beacon for others? The message here is clear: wishes, when nourished by actions and pure intentions, can indeed become reality. Perhaps it's time to stop seeing shooting stars as mere astronomical phenomena and start seeing them as symbols of infinite possibilities, ready to be realized through your positive will.

29.
The Unreachable Mountain:
Achieving High Goals

At the first light of dawn, Monk Akira paused to contemplate the Unreachable Mountain, whose peak seemed to pierce the sky like an arrow. Tales of ancient monks claiming the mountain was indomitable echoed through the monastery corridors. Its inaccessibility was almost a myth, an enigma no one had ever solved. Yet, Akira felt different that morning. He sensed that the distant and inaccessible mountain was somehow calling to him.

"We are made of the same matter, you and I," Akira whispered to the mountain, as if speaking to the universe itself. "I can climb it. I must climb it." With a sack containing only the essentials and a heart overflowing with determination, Akira began his journey.

In the courtyard of the monastery, the other monks watched Akira with expressions of disbelief and dismay. "He is mad," they murmured among themselves. "No one has ever succeeded in what he intends to do." But Akira smiled in the face of those glances and comments. Every look of doubt, every sigh of skepticism, became fuel for him, positive energy that fueled his resolve.

The climb was as arduous as the legends had predicted. Torrential rains lashed him, fierce winds tried to uproot him from the rocky walls, and there were moments when the path seemed truly insurmountable. On the steepest slopes, every inch gained seemed a miracle. Yet, with each challenge, Akira found new reserves of strength. "I am capable," he kept telling himself. "The mountain and I are one. If I surrender to it, I surrender to myself."

In moments of extreme discomfort, when his muscles screamed with fatigue and every fiber of his being seemed to beg to turn back, Akira closed his eyes and envisioned the peak. There, in the palace of his mind, he could see himself reaching that unattainable summit, and that thought made him invincible.

In the end, after what seemed like a lifetime of effort, Akira took the final step onto the summit. A sacred silence greeted him, and the world seemed to stretch out below him like a mantle of infinite possibilities.

Akira knew that, at that moment, he had done more than climb a mountain: he had climbed the depths of his being and emerged victorious.

Upon his return to the monastery, Akira found a different reception. The looks of doubt had been replaced by expressions of respect and admiration. He had not only conquered the Unreachable Mountain; he had conquered the spirits of those who doubted him and his resolve.

In Akira, they now saw a living exemplification of the strength of positive thinking and human tenacity.

With humility and grace, Akira shared his experience, emphasizing that each of them carried an "Unreachable Mountain" within themselves. "The true conquest," he said, "is not reaching the peak, but the journey that takes you there. And it's a journey that begins with a single step, fueled by faith in what is possible."

From that moment on, the monastery was never the same. Akira became a living legend, a tangible symbol of the power that resides in each of us when we dare to believe, when we dare to try, and when, above all, we dare to be positive.

Reflections

The story of Akira and the Unreachable Mountain is an effective and powerful metaphor for the inner journey each of us faces when setting seemingly unattainable goals.

Isn't it true that each of us has an "Unreachable Mountain" deep within our hearts? A desire or goal that seems so distant and unrealizable that it paralyzes us with its sheer imagination?

Akira faces his journey with determination, turning every doubt and skepticism into fuel that powers his resolution.

And you? How do you handle the doubt and skepticism that surround you? Have you ever considered the idea that these can be transformed into a positive power that strengthens your will?

Akira faces challenges that seem insurmountable. Torrential rains, fierce winds, and moments of extreme physical and mental discomfort. Yet, in every situation, he finds new reserves of strength. The key to his success? An unstoppable positive thought and a mental vision of his goal.

When you are put to the test, have you ever tried to close your eyes and vividly imagine your goal achieved? The power of positive visualization can be miraculous in its ability to transform reality.

Akira concludes his journey with wisdom that goes beyond the mere physical conquest of the mountain. He emphasizes that the true conquest is not the mountain peak, but the journey that leads you there. The same applies to you. It's not the achievement of the final goal that counts, but rather the person you become through the process of striving for it.

On a deeper level, Akira illustrates the importance of resilience, self-confidence, and belief in one's abilities. Have you ever wondered if just the act of firmly believing in yourself could actually enhance your capabilities? Akira conquers not just a mountain; he conquers himself and his untapped potential.

Finally, reflect on this: Akira's story also transforms the community around him. His success becomes a beacon of possibility for others. So it is also for you. Your personal achievements have the power to positively influence those around you, serving as inspiration and a demonstration of what is truly possible when we believe, try, and above all, stay positive.

Don't let your "Unreachable Mountain" remain an unattainable goal. Take that first, crucial step.

30.
The Light in the Dark:
Finding Positivity in Difficulties

It was a cold winter day when Monk Tenzin found himself standing before the entrance to a dark cave, a cavern whose terrible reputation had been passed down through generations in his village. The leaden sky seemed to threaten a storm, as if nature itself wanted to underscore the sense of melancholy surrounding the dark cavity. But Tenzin, a man with grizzled beard and piercing eyes, knew well that fear was often the child of ignorance. He had meditated enough on the nature of man and the universe to understand that even in the darkest darkness, there was always a light, however small, waiting to be discovered.

Before crossing the threshold of the cave, Tenzin stopped and focused, feeling the solid earth under his feet and the cold air on his face. With a certain solemnity, he lit a small beeswax candle. The flickering flames seemed to dance to the rhythm of his calm and measured breath. This small source of light became his beacon, and with it in hand, he ventured into the darkness.

Inside, every sensation was amplified immeasurably. The dripping of water from stalactites seemed to turn into a rhythmic drum, and every gust of wind from hidden cavities sounded like a mournful scream. Yet, each time his gaze fell on the candle, it seemed almost to whisper to him: "Go ahead, Tenzin, there is light even in the darkness. There is a greater intelligence that connects everything, and you are on the right path."

As he cautiously advanced, Tenzin noticed that the cave began to change. The path became more intricate, like the meanderings of the human mind, with nooks leading to dead ends and secret passages opening suddenly. In one of these moments of uncertainty, a hidden stone made him stumble, and the candle slipped from his hand, extinguishing instantly in its flight toward the ground.

Wrapped in total darkness, panic tried to envelop him like a dark cloud. But then, Tenzin closed his eyes and remembered the teachings on mindfulnes, self-reflection, and positive thinking.

He thought, "The candle is out, but the light, the real one, is also inside me." This realization freed him, and with trembling hands, he managed to relight the candle.

The flame now seemed brighter, as if fueled by his newfound confidence and determination. He continued to walk, and after what seemed like an eternity, he finally saw a glimmer of light in the distance. When he emerged from the cave, he found himself in a place of ineffable beauty, a secret garden in bloom, with lush trees and a sparkling lake, hidden from the world like an invaluable treasure.

That discovery illuminated his heart. Tenzin understood that the cave, fearsome and dark, was a passage to something wonderful, just like life's difficulties. Back at the monastery, he shared his experience with the other monks, and the secret garden became a sacred place of meditation. From that day on, the cave was no longer a place to avoid, but a passage to new understanding, a light in the dark that everyone could seek. Thus, the village learned that even in the darkest moments, there is always an exit, a glimmer of light, for those willing to look for it.

Reflections

The journey of Monk Tenzin through the dark cave is symbolic of a journey that each of us faces in life: the journey through difficulties, uncertainties, and fears that inevitably cross our path. Have you ever wondered why, when you are in the midst of your personal "caves," it seems that every sound is amplified, every fear accentuated?

Tenzin enters the cave with a small candle, a beacon of light and hope. It's not much different from the way you carry with you small glimmers of positivity and hope when facing your challenges. These glimmers might be an encouraging thought, a happy memory, or a motivational phrase.

But what happens when that candle is extinguished? When external circumstances blow away your source of light? In that moment of total darkness, Tenzin turns to his inner resources: he recalls past teachings, meditates to calm his mind, and finds the strength to move forward. It's a crucial moment for him, just as it is for you when you face your fears without obvious external aid. Can you find the light inside you even when everything seems dark?

The relighting of Tenzin's candle is not just a physical act but an act of renewed trust and determination. The darkness hasn't vanished, but the light seems brighter than ever. Have you ever felt this way? When, after a difficult trial, your inner strength reserve makes your subsequent steps more assured and your view clearer?

Finally, Tenzin discovers a secret garden, a place of peace and beauty beyond the darkness of the cave. It's not just a metaphor for the sense of accomplishment we feel when we overcome difficulties; it's also a reminder that every obstacle is a passage, not an end. Every one of your "caves" has an exit, a "secret garden" waiting to be discovered. Are you willing to look for it?

Tenzin's experience teaches that even in life's darkest moments, there's always a way out, a glimmer of light, if only we are willing to look for it. And just as Tenzin shared his wisdom with his village, you too have the opportunity to be a source of light for others.

31.
The Half-Full Chalice: Perspective Changes Everything

Every dawn at the Shōgen-ji monastery was a peaceful beginning, underscored by the melodious singing of birds and the sound of wood being struck to signal the start of prayers.
In this solemn yet comforting atmosphere, Monk Dogen engaged in a daily practice that had  become as sacred to him as it was mysterious to others.

It was a simple ritual, performed with intentionality and care. Dogen would approach the river flowing beside the monastery and, using a hand-carved crystal chalice, delicately scoop up the pure and clear water. The chalice was a work of art, a masterpiece by a local artisan who had etched into it designs of lotus flowers and dragons, symbols of purity and strength.

Back in his chamber, lit by the soft morning light filtering through rice paper panels, Dogen placed the chalice on a small altar. Then, sitting in the lotus position, he contemplated the chalice for a time that seemed suspended between the present and eternity. His eyes moved between the full and empty sides of the chalice, as if trying to balance a silent dance between yin and yang.

One day, the young novice Kaito, drawn by Dogen's ritual, paused at the threshold of the room. "Master Dogen, may I disturb your meditation for a question?"

Dogen opened his eyes and a smile appeared on his face. "Certainly, Kaito. What are you curious about?"

"Why, master, do you dedicate yourself to this chalice practice every day? Is it perhaps a reflection on impermanence, on the fragility of life?"

Dogen nodded, impressed by the depth of the novice's question. "Yes, Kaito, impermanence is certainly one aspect. But I want you to understand something more subtle. Every day, when I observe this chalice, I learn from its duality. Some might see the chalice as half empty, focusing on life's gaps, failures, and missed opportunities. Others, however, would see the chalice as half full, and in that half chalice, they would discover reasons for gratitude, optimism, and joy."

"Meditating on perspective can be more powerful than you might imagine. It can transform your interaction with the world and with yourself. The external reality remains unchanged, but the way you perceive it can turn your life into hell or heaven."

Kaito was awestruck, as if a veil had been lifted from his eyes. "Thank you, master. This is a lesson I will carry with me."

And so it was. From that day on, Kaito began to practice the chalice meditation. And not just him, but other monks and visitors to the monastery, influenced by the story of Dogen and Kaito, began to incorporate this practice into their lives. And they discovered, as Kaito did, that the simple act of focusing on the full side rather than the empty side could change not just the mood of a single day, but potentially the course of an entire life.

And Dogen, every morning, continued his practice, knowing that he had planted a seed, a small gesture that had grown into a garden of wisdom, where anyone could come to harvest the fruit of mindfulnes and gratitude.

Reflections

The tale of Monk Dogen and his crystal chalice is much more than a simple story of morning meditation; it's a profound lesson on the power of perspective. But what does it mean for you? Have you ever stopped to think about how often your view of things influences your reality? A chalice can be both half full and half empty, just as your life can be viewed through lenses of pessimism or optimism.

What do you see when you look at the "chalice" of your existence? Do you focus on the empty side, on the lacks, the obstacles, and the disappointments you've experienced? Or can you see the blessings, the opportunities, the beautiful experiences, and the moments of growth hidden in the full side of the chalice? Perspective is powerful; it can create insurmountable walls or open doors to new possibilities. Have you realized this?

Meditating on the duality of the chalice, as Dogen did, is an exercise that invites you to balance your view of life, to consider both the shadows and the lights of your journey. It's not just about choosing the full side for sheer optimism, but understanding that both aspects, full and empty, coexist. And in that balance, there's room for a new kind of mindfulnes, one that embraces the complexity of life without judgment.

Dogen emphasizes that perspective can transform not only how you interact with the external world but also your internal dialogue. It might seem hyperbolic, but think about how many moments of your life have been defined by how you interpreted a situation rather than the situation itself. Reality is largely a canvas on which we project our perceptions, beliefs, and attitudes. Have you ever wondered how much you could change your reality by changing your perspective?

And let's not forget the impact of the story on Kaito and the other monks. A single gesture, a single lesson, can have a chain effect, positively influencing many lives. What if you were next? A shift in perspective can not only improve your life but also serve as a beacon for others. What seed you plant today might grow into a garden of wisdom for you and those around you?

Perspective, as this story suggests, is a key to inner well-being and emotional balance. Sometimes, a shift in viewpoint is all it takes to see an entirely new world. It's a choice, and like all choices, it has the power to change everything.

32.
The Nest on the Peak:
Creating Your Own Paradise

In the remote and pristine mountain region of Kanchen, where snow-capped peaks seemed to touch the sky, stood an ancient monastery, wrapped in the silence of nature. The monastic community was small, composed of men and women dedicated to meditation and enlightenment. Among them, a monk named Senzo was particularly well-known. Not just for his deep wisdom and his way of life, but also for a habit as unique as it was mysterious.

At a certain distance from the monastery, grew an exceptional tree, a majestic sequoia, whose trunk was so thick it required five men to fully embrace it. Its roots sunk deep like arteries into the mother earth, while its branches extended in an ethereal embrace towards the sky. Every day, when the sun had just risen and the morning dew still wet the grass, Senzo would climb that tree.

One day, a visitor came to the monastery, drawn by the story of Senzo and the charm of the sequoia. After observing the monk's routine for some time, he couldn't help but ask, "Venerable Senzo, forgive my curiosity, but why do you climb so high up that tree? What do you hope to find or achieve up there?"

Senzo replied with a smile that radiated absolute tranquility: "I am building a nest at the top, my dear friend."

The visitor seemed incredulous. "A nest? Like that of a bird?"

"Exactly, but it's a nest for me. It's my little paradise."

Squinting against the sunlight, the visitor looked towards the top of the tree and noticed, indeed, a structure he hadn't seen before: a nest carefully and attentively built on the sturdy branches of the sequoia. It was a harmonious assembly of intertwined branches, green leaves, colored feathers, and blades of grass.

"But, Venerable Senzo, isn't it dangerous? It must be uncomfortable," the visitor couldn't help but ask.

With a reassuring tone, Senzo explained: "Danger and discomfort, my friend, are often a matter of perspective. When I'm up there, I feel close to the sky, away from the noise of the world, from distractions and worries. I find a kind of peace and serenity that isn't easily replicable elsewhere."

"But why a nest?" The visitor was visibly perplexed.

Senzo took a pause and continued: "You see, a nest is something very personal, a creation that reflects who you are and what you value. I built my paradise up there not because I despise the world below or find it unfit. On the contrary, it's because I desire a place that is exclusively the product of my positive thought, a place where every branch, every leaf, and every blade of grass represents a conscious choice."

Struck by this revelation, the visitor felt as if a veil had been lifted from his understanding. "So, in a way, you're saying that paradise is a personal construction, shaped by our perspective and attitude?"

"Exactly," said Senzo, "and don't forget, each of us has the capacity to build our own paradise, it's just a matter of choosing where and how."

From that day on, the story of Senzo and his nest on the peak became one of the most beloved and shared legends in the monastery and among pilgrims who came from faraway lands.

The intrinsic wisdom in his simple yet profound act served as a constant reminder: paradise is not a place to find, but a state of being to create.

And in the construction of this state of being, every choice of materials is actually a choice of life.

Reflections

Have you ever thought that paradise is not a physical place to reach, but a state of being to construct with your own hands?

The story of Senzo, the monk who built his nest at the top of a sequoia, offers an answer wrapped in deep wisdom.

Senzo teaches us that paradise is a personal construction, shaped by our perspective and attitude. It's not a distant destination, but a possible reality, here and now. The nest on the peak is a powerful symbol. It invites you to reflect on what it means for you to "be high up," away from the noise of the world.

In what place in your life, mental or physical, are you building your "nest"?

Is it a place made of positive thoughts and conscious choices?

Reflect on this: the nest that Senzo builds is not a place of escape but rather a tangible expression of his inner self. Every branch, every leaf, every blade of grass in his nest is a conscious choice, an embodiment of his values and desires.

How are you weaving the branches and leaves of your life?

Are they the fruit of conscious and careful choices, or rather of automatism and habits?

Danger and discomfort are often a matter of perspective.

What do you consider dangerous or uncomfortable on your path to building your personal paradise?

Is it the fear of others' judgment, the fear of failure, or perhaps the fear of discovering parts of yourself that you would prefer to ignore?

And what if these "dangers" were instead opportunities to grow, to become more authentic, to live in harmony with yourself and the world around you?

Lastly, Senzo reminds us that paradise is a state of being to create. It's not an unattainable utopia, but a reality within everyone's reach. And to build it, you must be the architect of your life. You must make conscious choices that reflect who you are and what you value.

How might you start building your nest, your personal paradise today?

What are the "materials" you would choose to weave your well-being and serenity?

Senzo's lesson is clear and universal: paradise is not a place to find, but a state of being to create. And every choice, every step, every thought is a milestone on your journey toward creating this paradise.

33.
The Favorable Wind:
Navigating Life with Optimism

The Jin monastery was like a little earthly paradise, enveloped in the scents of flowers and the melodic sound of birdsong. The monks engaged in morning prayers and philosophical debates, and dedicated themselves to monastic tasks like copying sacred texts and cultivating gardens. But for Jin, the true sanctuary was the lake that gently kissed the monastery's feet.

It was a large body of water, whose waters seemed to reflect the essence of the sky. Jin was not just a monk; he was also a navigator of the soul. Every day, regardless of his commitments, he found time to retreat to that place of peace. There, he had a boat, not particularly luxurious or large, but stable and safe.

When Eiichi joined him that day, he was immediately struck by the atmosphere of serenity that enveloped the boat. There were no superfluous ornaments, just a pair of oars, a sail, and a small votive altar dedicated to Kannon, the goddess of mercy.

"Come aboard, Eiichi," invited Jin with a smile that radiated a calm but intensely lively energy. "Today will be a special day."

As soon as Eiichi set foot on the boat, Jin moved skillfully, hoisting the sail that immediately swelled, capturing the wind as if it were a secret whispered by the sky. The experience was euphoric. The water gently lapped the sides of the boat, and the two monks were enveloped in a sensation of infinite freedom.

As they were far from the shore, Eiichi, overwhelmed by curiosity, couldn't help but ask: "How do you do it, Jin? How do you know the wind will always be in your favor?"

Jin smiled, gazing at the horizon as if he could read nature's secrets. "Eiichi, the wind is like life. I cannot control it, but I can decide how to react to it. My sail is my will, and my compass is my optimism. With these two allies, every wind can become favorable."

"I still don't understand," admitted Eiichi, a bit frustrated.

Jin slowed the boat and brought it into a small bay, where the water was so clear they could see the bottom. "Look down there, what do you see?"

"Stones, algae, small fish," listed Eiichi.

"Exactly. Each of them has a role in the grand scheme of life. Some stones may seem like obstacles, but they could also be solid foundations on which to build. Algae may seem insignificant, but they provide shelter to fish. Obstacles are just masked opportunities, Eiichi. When the wind blows against you, it's not a signal to give up; it's an invitation to learn, to readjust, and to find new directions."

The light in Eiichi's eyes changed, as if a deeper understanding had touched him. "So, if I understand correctly, you navigate not only on the lake but also through life, with the same philosophy."

"Exactly," confirmed Jin, "and now that you have tasted the favorable wind, perhaps you'll want to join me more often. Because, you see, we are never alone in this journey. Like the wind and the water, we are all connected, all part of an infinite flow that invites us to navigate, always, toward new and wonderful horizons."

And from that day on, Eiichi became a frequent companion of Jin on his excursions on the lake, both moved by the same spiritual breeze, both in search of their own personal favorable wind. And as Jin had taught him, he discovered that the secret was not so much in finding the right wind, but in being open and ready to sail, regardless of where it blew.

Reflections

Navigating life requires more than just a boat and a sail; it requires a deep understanding of the wind that surrounds us, which can be as changeable as life itself. The story of Jin and Eiichi invites you to consider a crucial question: how do you face the adverse winds of your existence? Do you oppose them with resistance, letting yourself be carried adrift, or do you learn to adjust your sail and use your inner compass to turn the wind into an ally?

Start to see your will as the sail of the boat. Every time you feel pushed by events, it's you who decides how to position that sail. You can leave it lowered and remain still, motionless, a victim of circumstances. Or you can hoist it confidently, letting the wind take you to new experiences. Have you noticed how your will can transform seemingly adverse circumstances into opportunities for growth and change?

But a sail without a compass is of little use. Here comes your optimism into play. Jin's compass is not a physical object, but a mindset. It's a system of beliefs that allows him to see not only challenges but also the opportunities they bring. And you, what beliefs reside deep in your soul? Do they open a world of possibilities or confine you to a corner?

Observe the tranquil bay in the story, where the water is so clear you can see to the bottom. Jin uses this moment to show Eiichi, and you, that obstacles are not always what they seem. Stones, algae, and fish coexist in a delicate balance. How many times have you considered an obstacle as a problem, when in reality it could be a springboard for something greater? How many times have you assumed that a problem was a sign to give up, instead of a challenge to face and overcome?

Jin's navigation on the lake is a spiritual journey, a microcosm of life itself. Every time he embarks, it's not just to traverse the waters but also to navigate through the complexities of existence. The same applies to you. Every day is an opportunity to hoist your sail and adjust your compass. And remember, life is not a solitary journey. Just as Eiichi found a companion in Jin, you too can find or become a companion for someone else, navigating together towards ever brighter horizons.

IV
Inner Peace

The Secret Sanctuary:
Build Your Inner Refuge

34.

The Silent Temple:
The Quiet of Calmness

In a bustling city, where the clang of vendor's bells mingled with children's laughter and the animated conversations of the elderly, there stood a temple. The Silent Temple, it was called. It was like an island amidst a stormy sea, a rare sanctuary of peace in a world ruled by chaos.

Yuudai, a monk with a heart pure and eyes wide open like lotus flower petals, was journeying in search of new wisdom. As he navigated through the market, his spirit sensed a strange attraction, like an anchor finding its perfect mooring. Following this inner call, he found himself before the ancient temple. He couldn't resist; it was as if the temple's quiet had called him by name.

Crossing the temple's threshold, Yuudai was enveloped in a silence so dense it seemed touchable, as if he could reach out and feel it. He sat on a meditation cushion and closed his eyes, immersing in that calmness as if it were a crystal-clear lake. For a few moments, everything else faded away. It was just him and the quiet, a sacred meeting of two entities separate yet equally real. "How can such deep quiet exist alongside the world's clamor?" he wondered, in awe.

When he opened his eyes and left the temple, Yuudai felt reborn. It was as if he had found a precious jewel and decided to carry it in his heart. He returned to the market, but this time it was different. The hustle and bustle of the outside world seemed to have lost its power to disturb him; his soul had become a waveless lake, indifferent to external storms.

A tea seller, an old man with a beard as white as snow and eyes as piercing as an eagle, noticed this change in Yuudai. "How do you maintain your calm in such a lively and noisy place?" he asked, pouring a cup of steaming tea.

Yuudai took the cup, savoring the tea's fragrance as if it were another sign of peace to add to his inner collection. Then he smiled, a smile that seemed to illuminate his entire being. "The temple I visited is not just a building of stone and wood, but an inner temple I can carry with me. And in that inner temple, there is always silence and peace."

The seller nodded, as if he had just received an answer to a lifelong tormenting question. He took a deep breath, and in that moment, he too felt a glimmer of the peace Yuudai had found. "Perhaps, after all," he thought, "quiet is not a place, but a state of mind that we all can achieve."

And so, Yuudai continued his journey, carrying with him the precious gift of quietness. But what he perhaps did not know was that he had left something even more precious behind: the realization that calm is a choice, a temple that each one can build within themselves, regardless of the external chaos.

Reflections

Have you ever wondered how some people manage to maintain their calm even amidst a frenetic environment? How they seem to have an indestructible aura of serenity despite the cacophony of the outside world? Perhaps, like Yuudai, they have discovered the secret of the inner "Silent Temple."

The temple we speak of is not physical, but a spiritual entity, a dimension of your consciousness that you can cultivate and carry with you wherever you go.

Ask yourself: "What is my Silent Temple? Where is my inner sanctuary of peace and tranquility?" Seeking this temple is like searching for a soulmate for your spirit.

Yuudai, in our story, represents the inner traveler in each of us, that spiritual seeker in search of wisdom and peace.

The silence and peace Yuudai found are not merely a physical retreat from the world, but rather an inner transformation. "How can I incorporate this quiet into my daily life?" you might ask. The key is recognizing that your inner "Silent Temple" is a place you can access at any moment. It doesn't require a geographical location or ideal external conditions. It is a state of mind, a conscious choice.

Just as Yuudai found his calm, you can find yours.

"What daily practices could help me cultivate my inner calm?" Meditation, deep breathing, or simply taking a moment to savor a cup of tea, like the seller in the story, can be your tools.

But perhaps the greatest lesson of this story is that your state of inner calm is not just a gift for yourself, but also for others. Have you ever wondered how much of your being could positively influence the people around you? The tea seller had a revelation just by observing Yuudai. Your calm could be the temple someone else is searching for.

Finally, dear friend, reflect on this question: "If calm is a choice, why not make it now?" You can start building your "Silent Temple" right at this moment, regardless of the chaos that might surround you. Like Yuudai, you will have not only found a treasure to carry with you but also cast a stone into the lake of humanity, creating ripples of peace that might reach unexpected corners of the world.

35.
The Waveless Ocean:
The Depth of Inner Peace

Kyoshi, a monk of great wisdom, was known in his village not only for his erudition but also for the palpable tranquility that emanated from him. One day, he decided to spend time along the shore of a frothing ocean, far from the  frenetic life of the monastery and village.

He walked slowly, feeling the cool sand beneath his feet and the salt in the air. Each wave crashing onto the shore seemed to tell a story, a cycle of life in perpetual motion. Kyoshi stopped, his gaze fixed on the horizon where the sky kissed the ocean.

With each breaking wave, Kyoshi felt more immersed in the eternal rhythm of nature. And at that precise moment, a revelation flashed in his mind: beneath the ocean's surface, beyond the tumult and chaos of the waves, lay a world of absolute calm, an abyss of inner peace.

Sitting on the damp sand, Kyoshi rested his hands on his knees and closed his eyes. He meditated deeply, tuning his mindfulnes to the depth of the ocean of his mind. Thoughts came and went like waves, but beneath them, he touched such profound calm that it almost brought him to tears.

When he opened his eyes, it was as though he had journeyed through unexplored abysses, discovering hidden treasures of serenity. This calm was not an escape from life's storms, but a stable foundation upon which all his challenges and joys could dance.

A fisherman named Hiroshi, who had observed Kyoshi from a distance, was struck by the monk's peaceful radiance. Unable to contain his curiosity, he approached and asked, "Excuse me, master, how do you maintain such calm in a world so full of noise and disorder?"

Kyoshi opened his eyes and looked at Hiroshi, his gaze as tranquil as a still lake. "Dear Hiroshi, true peace is not the absence of storms, but the depth of calm that exists beneath the surface waves. Every wave originates from that depth and eventually returns to it. So it is with our thoughts and emotions. If we can touch that depth within us, we can navigate any storm with a serene heart."

Hiroshi listened, his eyes wide in a mix of awe and gratitude. It was as if, through Kyoshi's words, he had discovered a new continent within his being, a place of eternal peace from which he could always draw.

From then on, Hiroshi saw neither the ocean nor life in the same way. And whenever he felt overwhelmed, he would close his eyes and think of Kyoshi and the waveless ocean, finding in that memory an anchor for his turbulent soul.

Reflections

Have you ever felt the need to escape from the chaos of everyday life, longing for a corner of peace that always seems elusive?

How often have you sought that calm in the external, hoping that a place or a situation could offer you the serenity you crave?

The story of Kyoshi, the monk with unfathomable depth, invites you to look beyond the turbulent surface of your circumstances and dive into the vast ocean of your interiority.

Kyoshi finds his calm not by fleeing the world but by facing it with a centered heart. He walks along the ocean, and instead of being captivated only by the turbulent waves, he perceives the peaceful depth that lies beneath. That depth exists in you too, an inner sanctuary where every thought, emotion, or challenge can arise and vanish without disturbing your essence.

And like Kyoshi, you too have the ability to touch this sacred space. But how to reach it? Meditation, mindfulness, and acceptance are your boats on this inner journey. When you sit in silence, you allow your thoughts to flow like waves.

What happens if you don't try to stop them but simply observe? You'll discover that beneath the tumult lies an abyss of quietness, always present, waiting to be recognized.

The fisherman Hiroshi's question represents what many of us ask: "How can I be calm in such a hectic world?" Kyoshi's answer is enlightening, as it emphasizes that true peace is not the elimination of external disorder, but the discovery of internal order.

Isn't it liberating to know that you don't have to control the entire universe, but just know the tranquil core that already exists within you?

And you, like Hiroshi, can find this anchor for your turbulent soul. Every time life seems overwhelming, close your eyes and dive into your inner ocean. Can you feel it? That calmness is as much a part of you as the surface waves.

So, why not explore this depth today? Take a moment to sit in silence. Listen to your breath, feel your heart, and open the door to that part of you that is eternally peaceful. And once discovered, carry this treasure with you, like Kyoshi, knowing that calm is not a far-off place to reach, but an ever-accessible state of being.

Are you ready to take the first step towards discovering your waveless ocean?

36.
The Immovable Mountain:
The Peace that Surpasses Understanding

Under a star-dotted celestial blanket kissed by the first rays of the sun, Eijun, a monk with indefinable age but eyes as deep as the night, stood at the foot of a mountain so majestic it seemed a slumbering giant. With a rough wooden staff, carved with ancient mantras, and a bag containing only the essentials for an inner journey, he embarked on the rugged path leading to the summit.

Each step on this path seemed like a chapter of a sacred book written in the language of nature. The road was strewn with slippery rocks that appeared as deliberate obstacles to test his determination. After them came a twisted passage, a veritable jungle of intertwined tree roots like a tangle of doubts and fears each of us carries deep in our hearts. But Eijun, rather than being discouraged, felt increasingly invigorated. Each challenge seemed to infuse his being with greater strength, as if the obstacles were teachers in disguise, bestowing precious lessons.

Once at the top, Eijun placed his sacred staff aside and, like an ancient king laying down his crown, sat on a flat rock, smoothed by years of erosion and wind passage. With closed eyes, the monk inhaled deeply the crisp air, a mix of pine needle fragrances and alpine flowers. Immersed in this ethereal realm, his thoughts began to vanish, like clouds dissipating in a clear sky. It was as if the mountain itself shared with him its eternal, solid peace, a peace that eluded human definitions, beyond the reach of words.

After a period that could have been a second or a century, Eijun opened his eyes. He found himself the sole spectator of a natural theater, with the sky as a stage and the Earth as an audience. For the first time, he felt as if he were a small but precious note in a cosmic symphony that had no beginning or end.

Just then, a weathered but lively-eyed shepherd guiding his flock along the green slope of the mountain noticed Eijun. He felt irresistibly drawn to his aura of calmness and approached, like a moth to a flame.

"Excuse the interruption, oh monk. But what have you discovered atop this mountain that has rendered you so serene?" asked the shepherd, curiosity shining in his eyes.

With a smile resembling the sunrise, Eijun replied, "Dear friend, what I have found is a peace that cannot be captured by words. It's the peace that exists beyond the changing seasons and the tides of life. It's like this mountain: eternal, solid, and completely independent of everything that surrounds it."

The shepherd looked towards the peak, then back at Eijun, as if trying to grasp a concept just beyond his reach. "How can I find this peace, monk? I've searched, but it always seems to slip through my fingers."

Eijun placed his hand on the shepherd's shoulder. "This peace, my dear, is like a mountain hidden inside each of us. Yes, you will have to traverse arduous paths and face unexpected obstacles. But once you reach the summit, you'll discover that every step, every difficulty, was merely a milestone on the path to a peace that surpasses understanding."

The shepherd nodded, a shy but sincere smile crossing his face. He might not have fully grasped Eijun's words yet, but he knew he had felt something true, something that resonated deep within his being. And with that mindfulnes, both found their way back: one towards his flock, the other towards the solitude of the mountain, but both a bit closer to the inner peace they had always sought.

Reflections

The story of Eijun and the Immovable Mountain. A narrative that speaks to the heart and soul.

How often have you found yourself in difficult situations, treacherous paths that seem to challenge your determination? And how many times have you felt that each obstacle was an almost insurmountable test?

But reflect: are not these obstacles your greatest teachers? Isn't every slippery rock, every intertwined root a chapter in the story of your inner growth? Each of these moments shapes you, carves you, just as the wind and erosion have smoothed the rock on which Eijun found his moment of peace.

Have you ever thought about the eternal nature of the peace that Eijun discovered? It's not a peace conditioned by external events, but rather a peace that "surpasses understanding," existing beyond the changing seasons and life's tides.

Have you ever wondered if such peace might also exist within you?

Eijun discovers this monumental tranquility only after traversing the difficult path. You might wonder, is it necessary to face such challenges to discover your "inner mountain"? Perhaps the answer lies in understanding that peace is not a destination, but a journey. Every step you take, every obstacle you overcome, is but a milestone on the path to a peace that cannot be explained, only lived.

And you, like the shepherd, might feel irrevocably drawn to the quest for this peace. But how to reach it? Be willing to embark on your journey, to accept challenges and obstacles as precious lessons. And remember, this mountain is within you, hidden perhaps, but eternally present and immovable. Isn't this realization the first step towards the peace that surpasses understanding?

Reflect on this. Every difficulty, every obstacle you encounter is a necessary passage, a milestone bringing you ever closer to the summit of your inner mountain. And once you reach that summit, who can say what magnificent vistas await you? What unfathomable peace you might finally embrace? Isn't the prospect of such discovery the driving force behind your path, making every step, every moment, a progression towards the elusive?

37.
The Heart's Cave:
Intimacy with Oneself

Kiyoshi was a monk with a wandering spirit, a pilgrim of sacred and hidden places that nature had to offer. He had traversed forests as dense as labyrinths and forded rivers so tumultuous they seemed intent on swallowing the world. But that day, as he ventured along a mountain path shrouded in mist, a thrill of excitement ignited his heart.

Discovered almost by chance, nestled between moss-covered rocks and a complex web of roots, a cave unfolded before him. It wasn't just any cave; it radiated an aura of sacredness so palpable that Kiyoshi felt as though he had crossed a portal into another world.

Holding a lantern made of wood and rice paper, Kiyoshi made his way into the cave. The soft glow of the lantern revealed stone walls that seemed to embrace each ray of light, transforming it into a silent but tangible warmth. With reverence, he placed the lantern on a natural ledge and sat on a smooth boulder, perhaps shaped by millennia of erosion.

There, enveloped in the cloak of absolute silence, Kiyoshi felt as if every layer of his being had been gently lifted. It was as though he had passed through veils of illusion, penetrating the sanctum sanctorum of his heart. He began to meditate, each breath a journey inward, each exhalation a return to essence.

With the passage of time, or perhaps outside of time itself, Kiyoshi realized a simple but profound truth. The cave was an extension of his heart, a place not of escape, but of encounter. An encounter with himself, a dialogue without words or judgments. It was as if he had found a sacred place within himself, an inner altar where peace was not a guest but a resident.

And just as the lantern began to burn its final moments of light, Kiyoshi opened his eyes. The cave was immersed in darkness, but within him shone an inextinguishable light.

It was then that a shepherd named Hiroshi burst into the cave, panting and with a worried look. He had lost a sheep, and his wanderings had led him here.

"Forgive me, monk, I fear I have disturbed your sacred silence," Hiroshi whispered, a veil of apprehension in his voice.

Kiyoshi smiled with a serenity that seemed to flow from the heart of the earth itself. "True silence is not so easily disturbed."

Moved by that tranquility, Hiroshi asked, "How can I find such peace?"

Kiyoshi looked at him with kind eyes. "Every man has a cave in his heart. Sometimes life invites us to enter it, to discover that sacred place where the being reveals itself in its totality. Start there, Hiroshi. Find your sacred space, within or without, and embrace the magnificence of your authentic self."

The lesson was simple, yet as penetrating as the wind blowing through rock crevices, transforming everything in its path. Hiroshi nodded, thanked the monk, and set off, feeling that his search for the lost sheep had taken an unexpected but blessed turn.

Reflections

Have you ever wondered if you have found your sacred space, that inner place where you can be completely yourself without judgments or prejudices? Often we seek peace and serenity externally, in places or people, forgetting that the purest source of such peace resides within us.

Kiyoshi discovers, through his meditation in that sacred cave, that tranquility and understanding are not only to be sought in the external world.

Are you aware that you too possess a Heart's Cave? A place where you can retreat, away from the clamor of everyday life, to find your center? Do you also feel the need for a symbolic place where you can stop wearing the social masks that life forces you to bear?

Hiroshi's unexpected visit at the end of the story reminds us that life is full of interruptions and distractions. But how do you react to these obstacles?

Do they allow you to ruin your inner balance or, like Kiyoshi, have you learned that "True silence is not so easily disturbed"? Take a moment to reflect on this.

Do you allow yourself to be easily disturbed or have you found a balance that is unassailable?

The encounter with Hiroshi also reveals another teaching: it's not just about finding your sacred space but recognizing it as an extension of your deepest self. "Every man has a cave in his heart," says Kiyoshi. So, have you identified your sacred space? And if so, do you honor it as an extension of yourself?

Your sacred space is not just a place of refuge; it's a place of encounter with yourself, a dialogue without words or judgments.

Kiyoshi teaches us that inner peace is more than a condition or a state of mind; it's a place we can visit whenever we want. A place where we can be truly ourselves, free from every expectation and concern.

The story guides us toward a deeper understanding of positive thinking. It's not just about optimism or facing difficulties with a smile. It's about knowing and embracing your authentic nature, that part of you that is immutable even in the face of external changes.

When you are able to do this, like Kiyoshi, you will discover an inexhaustible source of light and peace that no external circumstance can tarnish.

In your Heart's Cave, you will find a peace that is uniquely yours, a treasure you can carry with you wherever you go.

Remember, true peace begins with being intimate with ourselves, in the most sacred and inviolable place we have: our heart.

38.
The Bamboo Forest:
The Flexibility of the Mind

I n a secluded valley, kissed by the sun and caressed by the winds, stood an ancient monastery. Haru, a young monk with a burning heart, was known for his unending quest for spiritual growth. One afternoon, after hearing an ancient parable, he decided to walk in the bamboo forest flanking the monastery. The forest was like a natural cathedral, where each bamboo stalk seemed a pillar erected in honor of the universe. The wind played sweet melodies there, as if every blade of grass was a string of a great cosmic instrument.

With every step, Haru felt his spirit rise. The ancient writings said that bamboo was a symbol of resilience and adaptability, and he wanted to absorb that wisdom into his meditative practice. He walked slowly, his bare feet feeling the softness of the ground, while the bamboo leaves cast a dancing shadow on the earth.

He stopped in front of a particularly tall bamboo stalk, swaying majestically in the breath of the wind. Unlike the robust but rigid trees he had seen succumb under the force of storms, this bamboo seemed to dance with the wind, bending but not breaking. It was as if it had understood the secret of balancing strength and flexibility.

Finding a flat rock near a small pond reflecting the azure sky like a mirror, Haru sat down. He crossed his legs and closed his eyes, sinking into deep meditation. He imagined himself as a bamboo stalk, his body and mind flexible yet strong, swaying with the winds of life's events, but never breaking. He felt an ethereal calm envelop him, and a revelation illuminated him like a lightning bolt in the sky: being flexible does not mean being weak; it means being strong enough to adapt without breaking.

When he opened his eyes, a new understanding shone within him. He observed the roots of the bamboo stalks, like fingers of the earth firmly anchored in the soil. He understood that their strength also lay in their stability; they were well-rooted in the earth, allowing them to be flexible without breaking. Like the bamboo, he too needed a solid foundation – of values, principles, and a deep sense of self – to dance with life.

It was at that moment that an elderly farmer named Taro entered the scene. He had come to collect bamboo shoots for his dinner. Noticing Haru in a meditative state, he was drawn to his aura of peace and approached.

"Excuse my intrusion, young monk," said Taro, his eyes filled with wisdom gained through the years. "May I know what has guided you to the heart of this enchanted forest?"

Haru opened his eyes and, smiling, replied: "I am here to listen to the teachings of the bamboo, which show me how to be strong and flexible on the journey of life."

Taro nodded sagely and added, "The bamboo is a silent but powerful teacher. It not only bends in the face of challenges but also finds ways to thrive where others yield. It is an emblem of our existence, showing us how to navigate through life's storms."

Thus, in the heart of the bamboo forest, Haru found a deeper understanding of himself and the delicate balance that governs all things.

Reflections

Have you ever walked in a bamboo forest, where each step is an embrace of the ground and the wind sings among the stalks?

Perhaps not, but you have certainly encountered storms in your life that have tested you, pushing you to seek that delicate balance between strength and flexibility. In Haru's story, there is a profound lesson about the elasticity of the mind, a concept that might be the key to navigating through your own storms.

Like Haru, have you ever wondered what it means to be flexible yet strong?

The story shows that flexibility is not a manifestation of weakness but rather a form of silent strength.

When life presents you with a storm, do you bend like the bamboo or break like a rigid tree? Are resilience and adaptability interwoven into your being, ready to emerge when you face adversity?

The bamboo offers a sublime metaphor for this lesson. It manages to bend in the wind without breaking, thanks to its roots firmly anchored in the ground.

How can you anchor yourself to face the storms that life inevitably brings to each of us? Perhaps it is through a set of unmovable values, or perhaps through a deep mindfulnes of who you are. Without these roots, flexibility could turn into fragility.

Are you aware of your "roots," those beliefs and principles that give you the strength to be flexible?

The lesson that Haru and, by extension, each of us can learn from the bamboo forest is both simple and profound. Being flexible yet strong, capable of bending but not breaking, are qualities that not only help us navigate life's storms but also find lasting inner peace.

The story of the bamboo is a powerful metaphor that invites you to reflect on the elasticity of your mind.

Being like bamboo is an act of balance: the strength to endure, the flexibility to adapt, and the wisdom to discern the right moment for each.

And in this mindfulnes, you will find the ability not only to face life's storms but also to thrive through them.

39.
The Lotus Lake:
The Beauty of Simplicity

In a land not so far away, where monasteries served as rare havens in a turbulent world, Kaito found himself confused and overwhelmed by the dogmas and rituals of the monastery in which he lived. The stone walls, ancient scriptures, and complex Buddhist teachings seemed to form a barrier that prevented him from finding the hidden truth within himself.

His master, the wise Monk Takeshi, noticed his pupil's furrowed brow during meditation sessions. With penetrating eyes, etched with the seasons of countless autumns, Takeshi saw beyond appearances. "Kaito, your mind seems like a stormy forest. Perhaps it's time to seek stillness. Go to the Lotus Lake. Listen to what the wind and water have to say."

Gratefully accepting the advice, Kaito donned his straw sandals and set out on the dirt path leading to the lake. As he walked, the birdsong and rustling leaves seemed to form a chorus inviting him to free his mind. But it was only when he reached the edge of the Lotus Lake that the true spectacle revealed itself before his eyes.

The lake was like a vast mirror of water, reflecting the blue sky dotted with white clouds. Lotus flowers floated on the surface like elegant dancers, in a silent choreography that only nature could orchestrate. Kaito crouched by the shore, touching the fresh, damp grass with his hands as if to caress the Earth itself.

He took a deep breath, inhaling the essence of the place. When he opened his eyes, he was drawn to a single lotus flower that seemed to shine brighter than the others. "What is your secret?" he whispered. As if the lake and the flower had been waiting for that moment, Kaito felt a wave of understanding wash away his worries.

The truth was there, in the lotus flower: an impeccable representation of grace, unencumbered by complexity.

It was then that Hiroshi, a fisherman whose boat was like a small floating island of wisdom, echoed his thoughts: "The lotus, anchored in the mud but reaching for the light, is a silent teacher. It shows that even in the murky waters of life, we can find our own light."

Kaito returned to the monastery, but this time with a renewed heart. The ancient scriptures, rituals, and ceremonies were no longer chains but bridges to a deeper understanding. Thanks to the lesson learned from nature, Kaito had finally found his way to live in the here and now, celebrating the beauty of simplicity.

Reflections

The story of Kaito at the Lotus Lake is one of those pearls of wisdom that invite you to suspend judgment, for a moment, on everything you know or think you know.

Have you ever felt overwhelmed by details, obstacles, or dogmas surrounding you? How many times have you found yourself in a situation like Kaito's, where the complexities of life seemed to obstruct your view of the simplest and purest truth?

The monastery, with its solid stone walls and intricate teachings, symbolizes any environment or belief that, rather than guiding you, confuses you.

Have you ever wondered if the tools you use to seek the truth are actually obscuring the truth itself?

Like Kaito, perhaps you too need to step away for a moment, to find a place or an inner space that allows you to see clearly.

The Lotus Lake acts as a powerful symbol of this purity and simplicity. Think about your 'version' of this lake.

Where do you feel most at ease? Is it a physical place or an inner space known only to you?

As you meditate on this, imagine touching that fresh, damp grass, savoring the air, and being welcomed by that single lotus flower that shines brighter than the others. What simple truth is it revealing to you?

The lotus flower, growing in the mud yet striving towards the light, shows you that beauty and simplicity can be found even in the most challenging circumstances. "Even in the murky waters of life, we can find our own light," says Hiroshi, the fisherman.

So, what is your 'murky water'? And how can you touch your own light even when you're immersed in it?

When Kaito returns to the monastery, his perspective has changed. The ancient scriptures and rituals are no longer chains but bridges to a deeper understanding. You too, armed with the lesson learned from the lotus flower, might discover that the same things that once seemed like obstacles are actually tools bringing you closer to your purest essence.

The beauty of simplicity is an open door to inner peace, a door that we all can choose to walk through. Like the lotus flowers floating on the lake, so too can we find a sense of peace and purpose in the simplicity that we often overlook but is always available to us.

So, the next time you feel oppressed by the complexities of life, remember the Lotus Lake. For there is nothing more liberating than discovering that the truth has always been there, in the beauty of simplicity, just waiting for you to see it.

40.
The Zen Garden:
The Harmony of Order and Chaos

Masaru was a monk with a burning passion, always in pursuit of perfection. In the quiet monastery where he lived, he was designated as the keeper of the sacred Zen garden, a task he accepted with reverence and solemnity. Every morning, as the first breath of light crossed the sky, Masaru was already up, bent in contemplation over the stones and sand of the garden. With a fine-toothed rake, he meticulously drew wavy lines in the ground, forming intricate patterns representing the ebb and flow of the universe.

However, nature had a mind of its own. Each day, the wind played with the sand, transforming the orderly lines into a kaleidoscope of unexpected shapes. Birds, in a whim of freedom, took twigs and dropped them on the ground, and dried leaves from surrounding trees fell like autumn snowflakes, disrupting the harmony that Masaru had created with such devotion.

One morning, frustration reached its peak. "Why," Masaru sighed, "can't I maintain perfect order? Am I insufficient as the guardian of this sacred space?"

Master Anzu, with eyes deep as wells of wisdom, had noticed the turmoil of his disciple. He approached Masaru and placed a hand on his shoulder. "What troubles your spirit, my young friend?"

Masaru looked at the master and said with a voice laden with confusion, "No matter how hard I try, Master, the garden escapes my control. It seems to have a will of its own, rebelling against my pursuit of order."

Anzu smiled, his face as relaxed as a calm lake. "Have you ever thought," he gently said, "that true harmony might reside precisely in the balance between the order you try to establish and the chaos nature spontaneously offers you?"

Those words penetrated Masaru's soul like a drop of water in a still lake, creating growing ripples of understanding.

He sat in the middle of the garden, setting aside his rake, and meditated. For the first time, he opened himself to the possibility that order and chaos might not be opposing forces, but complementary. And as if he had just opened a window, he felt a gentle breeze caress his face, like a sign of approval from the cosmos.

From that moment, his approach to gardening changed. He no longer sought to dominate nature but to dance with it. He began to see the fallen leaves as treasures offered by the season, and the play of the wind on the sand as the touch of an invisible artist, adding an element of surprise and beauty to his work.

The inner peace Masaru so desperately sought no longer came from the need to exert absolute control, but from accepting and harmonizing the divergent energies that form the tapestry of life. His garden transformed into a microcosm of this eternal wisdom, a sanctuary inviting every visitor to discover balance in the eternal dance between order and chaos, between action and acceptance.

And so, like the petals of a flower opening to embrace the sunlight, Masaru and his garden became one entity, a living symbol of the harmony that can arise when we embrace all parts of ourselves and the world around us.

Reflections

Have you ever wondered how much control you need to exercise to have a harmonious life?

Perhaps, like Masaru, you've tried to order every aspect of your life, only to find that some elements seem to escape your control.

What if the key to a harmonious life lies in your ability to dance with chaos rather than trying to stifle it?

Masaru's story offers an important lesson on the concept of balance. It's not just about creating an atmosphere of perfection and order; it's equally vital to recognize and accept the inherent chaos that life presents us.

Have you ever considered that perhaps obstacles, uncertainties, and even your imperfections could be your greatest teachers?

Initially, Masaru tried to maintain a perfectly ordered Zen garden, but every day nature introduced elements of disorder: the wind, birds, falling leaves. Does this happen to you too?

Have you noticed that no matter how much you may try to plan or control, there will always be factors outside your control?

But are you really inadequate if you can't keep everything perfectly under control?

The turning point for Masaru comes when Master Anzu suggests that true harmony might lie in the balance between the order he seeks and the chaos life offers.

And you, have you ever thought that it might be precisely in accepting and integrating these opposites that you find your inner peace?

Masaru finds a new form of balance when he stops fighting nature and starts dancing with it. You can do the same. Instead of trying to eliminate every element of uncertainty or difficulty from your life, try to see them as opportunities to grow and learn. They might be the touches of an "invisible artist," adding depth and beauty to your existence.

So, what would your dance with life look like?

How can you harmonize the seemingly contrasting forces of your inner and outer world?

What if the obstacles you encounter are not barriers to your happiness but rather cornerstones on which to build a more complete and satisfying life?

Masaru discovers that true peace comes from harmonizing the divergent energies that make up the tapestry of life. And you too can find your unique form of balance, accepting all aspects of yourself and the world around you.

As we walk through the garden of our existence, we can learn from Masaru and his Zen garden. We can find our inner peace not in rigid control but in balance: a balance that welcomes and unifies order and chaos in a harmonious embrace.

So, like Masaru, you too, dear reader, can find your peace in the harmony that unites opposites, in the delicate balance that makes life a Zen garden of infinite beauty.

How?

The answer, as Masaru discovers, might be as simple as it is profound: not to resist, but to dance.

41.
The Still River:
Patience as a Virtue

It was a day wrapped in celestial calm when Monk Yuki, dressed in his usual robe, ventured into the wooded paths surrounding the ancient monastery. The leaves of the trees moved gently to the rhythm of the wind, as if dancing to the melody of silence. But it was the river, that river he had seen countless times, which caught his attention like never before. The river, usually gracefully weaving its waters among the rocks, seemed to have paused.

"What strange enchantment is this?" thought Yuki, both fascinated and troubled. The waters, which had always been a symbol of perpetual motion, seemed to have found a moment of pure, unexpected stillness.

Deeply intrigued, Yuki returned to the monastery – the pulsating heart of ancient wisdom – and sought out Master Hakuin. He found him in the Zen Garden, intent on drawing circles in the sand with a long bamboo stick. "Master, why does the river that has always danced like the wind today lie silent as the night? Is it not the nature of water to flow?"

Master Hakuin looked up, his penetrating eyes seeming to peer into Yuki's soul. "Yuki, how many times have we observed the moon reflected in that river? And yet, we have never seen the same river twice. Beneath that veil of apparent immobility, millions of water droplets perform their invisible dance. Patience is like that: it may seem a tranquil lake, but beneath the surface is a current of strength and determination."

The wisdom in Master Hakuin's words echoed in Yuki's heart like a bell in a silent valley. Yuki began to meditate daily on the banks of that enigmatic river. He not only observed the surface but closed his eyes to hear the secrets the river whispered: the subtle gurgle of water against stones, the delicate songs of birds flying low. Each sound spoke to him of the hidden complexity behind simplicity, of strength masked by calm.

"Patience is indeed like this water," reflected Yuki. "In it lies a silent force, a resilience that overcomes every obstacle with disarming equanimity. It is the silent engine that fuels my quest for inner peace."

Over time, Yuki's serene composure became legendary within the ancient walls of the monastery. Even the younger monks began to notice an almost ethereal luminosity emanating from him, a light that only profound inner peace can bestow. Yuki became a source of inspiration, sharing his discovery as a precious gem: "Patience is not just a virtue; it is an art. An art that, once mastered, makes us sculptors of our soul, capable of carving an inner sanctuary where serenity resides."

And so, in every lesson he imparted, in every conversation he had, Yuki reminded himself and others of the lesson of the still river: that patience, in its seemingly static being, is a wonderfully ordered chaos of forces at play, an eternal dance of water and time teaching us to flow gracefully through the meanders of life.

Reflections

Has there ever been a moment in your life when you felt like the river in Yuki and Master Hakuin's tale? A time when, outwardly, everything seemed to have stopped, when you became a static lake instead of a flowing river? Sometimes, our life seems to freeze in apparent immobility, creating an internal tension that tests our patience.

Perhaps you've asked yourself: "Why am I not moving forward? Where has my energy gone?" Yet, just as Yuki discovered through Master Hakuin's wisdom, beneath the calm surface hides a world of activity and movement.

Patience is silent dynamism. It is a river flowing under a seemingly immobile surface, charged with potential and strength.

Have you ever stopped to consider that patience might not be mere waiting but intentional activity? It's not giving up but an act of faith in life's invisible dance. It's like the circles in the Zen Garden's sand drawn by Master Hakuin: simple on the surface, yet deeply meaningful in their essence.

So, what does it really mean to master the art of patience? It means developing a quiet resilience that allows you to face obstacles and adversity with stoic calm. It means observing reality, recognizing its nuances, and acting appropriately. Just as Yuki became a beacon of wisdom and composure, you can become a guardian of your own serenity.

How can you apply this lesson in your daily life?

You might start with a deep meditation exercise, perhaps in a natural setting that inspires you. Close your eyes and imagine a river inside you. Listen to its flow, recognize its subtle sounds, and discover its hidden dance. Observe your patience as Yuki observed the river: as an element of strength and determination masked by calm.

On your journey toward inner growth, patience will be your most faithful companion. The question then is: are you ready to learn the silent dance that fuels the art of patience? Are you willing to let it become the silent engine of your quest for inner peace?

Remember, like the still river, your patience is a wonderfully ordered chaos of forces at play. And in its quiet, there is an inner movement, an eternal dance inviting you to flow gracefully through life's meanders.

42.

The Eagle's Flight:
The Importance of Detachment

Toshiro, the young monk, climbed the mountain overlooking the valley, where the ancient walls of the monastery contrasted with the surrounding green pastures. From that summit, the world seemed like a miniature painting, and the wind carried echoes of monastic chants and leaves dancing in the air.

As his gaze wandered, it caught the majestic figure of an eagle soaring high in the sky. The eagle's wings were spread wide, almost caressing the ascending currents of the wind. Yet, despite its altitude and distance from the ground, the bird emanated a sense of imperturbable serenity.

Toshiro felt mesmerized. "How does this eagle soar with such lightness and indifference, at a midpoint between heaven and earth, between the sacred and the profane?" he wondered. It was at that moment that a revelation illuminated his spirit. The eagle could be free and serene because its flight was an exercise in detachment, a liberation from the bonds of the world below.

Returning to the monastery, Toshiro immediately sought out his Master Hikaru. "Master," he began fervently, "I observed an eagle soaring in the sky and understood that detachment is the key to viewing the world with unclouded eyes. How can I live with this kind of freedom and peace?"

Master Hikaru's face lit up with a gentle smile as he sagely replied, "Ah, the eagle! It does not fret about the storms raging beneath its wings or the hostile winds trying to divert it. It rises above all that. Similarly, detachment allows you to be above the emotional storms and conflicts that characterize earthly life."

Toshiro treasured his master's words. In the days and weeks that followed, whenever he felt overwhelmed by emotions or circumstances, he closed his eyes and imagined himself as that eagle. He felt as if his spiritual wings were lifting him above the tumult, allowing him to view the situation with new clarity.

"I am not obliged to react to every stimulus or disturbance," he reflected. "I can choose to be an observer, to be free from bonds that would have dragged me down."

And Toshiro learned that detachment is not synonymous with coldness or disinterest. On the contrary, it is a form of wisdom that allows you to interact with the world in a more authentic and loving way.

Over time, his calmness and clarity became legendary among his fellow monks. He shared with them the secret of the eagle's flight, teaching that detachment is not an escape but an ascent; not a withdrawal but a higher form of engagement.

Reflections

How do you rise above daily challenges, emotional tumult, and the incessant noise of life? Have you ever felt overwhelmed by stress or worries, unable to see the bigger picture?

The story of Toshiro and the eagle offers an enlightening answer: the power of detachment.

Imagine being that eagle, soaring between heaven and earth at a dizzying height. It is there that the eagle finds a point of equilibrium, allowing it to fly freely despite winds and storms.

What if you could do the same? What if you could rise above your circumstances, observing life from a higher perspective?

Detachment is not a withdrawal from the world or a form of disinterest. It is rather a state of freedom that allows you to interact with the world in a more authentic way. Think of all the times when emotions or situations have dragged you down, negatively affecting your peace or well-being.

What would change if, instead of reacting impulsively, you gave yourself a moment to rise spiritually, like the eagle?

This kind of detachment is a double gift. On the one hand, it offers you the freedom not to be governed by passing emotions or difficult circumstances. On the other, it allows you to face these same issues with greater clarity and wisdom. Toshiro found in the figure of the eagle a guide for his spiritual path, something you could do too.

What could change in your life if you embraced such a perspective?

But how can we practice detachment in everyday life? Start with mindfulnes. Every time you feel overwhelmed or bogged down, take a pause. Close your eyes and imagine being that eagle, free and serene, observing the situation from above. This will allow you to see not just the details but also the bigger picture, enabling you to act rather than react.

And again, what if detachment was the key to a higher form of engagement with the world?

Detachment is not a retreat, but rather a deeper immersion into reality. It is a form of wisdom that makes you capable of love and compassion precisely because you are free from the bonds that would have dragged you down.

And so, I invite you to consider the eagle's flight as a symbol of detachment and freedom. Do not let yourself be imprisoned by emotional storms or life's pressures. Rise, like the eagle, and you will find unparalleled peace and clarity.

As always, the key to a serene life is in your hands; you just need to open them and let the wind carry you aloft.

43.
The Rose and the Thorn:
Accepting the Sweet and the Bitter

In the deep silence of twilight, Kaito found himself once again in the enchanted garden of the monastery. The golden lights of sunset illuminated the leaves, while the scent of roses permeated the air, caressing the senses like an ancient melody. His step was light, as if he were walking on a cloud.

He touched the velvety petals of a rose again, that emblem of ephemeral beauty. It was as if the flower whispered stories of love and passion, of things that bloom and then wither. This time, with a deeper mindfulnes, he gently held the flower between his fingers. The prick of the thorns was an immediate reminder, a minor wound speaking of an eternal truth.

Kaito, still holding the rose, went to the tea room where Master Takeshi was preparing ceremonial matcha. The room radiated an aura of calm, each object and movement seeming to be part of a sacred dance. "Master Takeshi," Kaito exclaimed, opening his palm to show the small wound, "why does life give us moments of ecstasy only to counter them with moments of suffering?"

Takeshi poured the green tea with steady hands, his eyes wells of wisdom. "You see, the thorns are guardians of beauty," he began. "They are not there to punish you, but to teach you. Every rose has its thorns, just as every day has its night. They are not oppositions, but complements."

Kaito listened, fascinated, as the master continued: "You can enjoy the scent of the rose only if you are willing to risk the prick of its thorns. Similarly, the bitter taste of the tea we are drinking enhances its intrinsic sweetness."

In the days that followed, Kaito discovered new levels of acceptance. He met the joys and pains of life not as antagonists, but as silent teachers. He began to see difficulties as opportunities to grow, and moments of joy as sacred spaces of gratitude and humility.

One morning, while teaching the novices, Kaito used the rose as a symbol in a lesson. "Every experience, beautiful or ugly, is a petal on this rose that is life. Do not shun the thorns, but appreciate them for what they are: messengers of wisdom that help you value the beauty of the petals."

Over time, Kaito's wisdom spread well beyond the monastery's ancient walls. People came from far away to hear his words. And each time he spoke, it was as if an invisible rose bloomed in the heart of the listener, a perfect balance of sweet and bitter that illuminated the path to inner peace.

Reflections

What does the rose represent for you? And the thorns?

How many times in your life have you touched one, admired its beauty, and felt the prick of its thorns?

In this story, Kaito discovers a fundamental truth that applies to all of us: life is a dance between the sweet and the bitter, between pleasure and pain. Have you ever realized this?

Have you ever thought that your ability to appreciate life's beauty might be directly proportional to your willingness to accept its difficulties?

Master Takeshi offers not just tea to Kaito; he offers wisdom.

"The thorns are guardians of beauty," he says. They are not there to harm us, but to teach us. This concept reveals a profound level of mindfulnes.

Have you ever wondered how your life might change if you saw challenges and difficulties as "guardians of beauty" rather than obstacles to overcome?

Takeshi continues, emphasizing that the sweet and the bitter, pleasure and pain, are not in opposition but are complementary. Just as the bitter taste of tea enhances its sweetness, so too can moments of suffering give resonance to the moments of joy in your life. Have you ever noticed how happy moments often follow periods of struggle? And have you ever thought that it might be those difficulties that make such moments so sweet?

Kaito, then, integrates this wisdom into his daily life. He views every experience, both beautiful and ugly, as a petal on a rose. And you? Have you ever tried to see your experiences in this way? If you could see every challenge as an opportunity for growth and every moment of happiness as a chance for gratitude and humility, how would your perspective on life change?

The story of Kaito invites us to explore a form of positive thinking that goes beyond mere optimism or avoidance of pain. It's not about always looking for the "silver lining" but about accepting every aspect of life as a silent teacher that can help us grow.

Does this seem like an achievable goal to you? And if so, how might it impact your journey towards greater mindfulnes and well-being?

You don't need to live in a monastery or participate in a tea ceremony to apply these teachings. Just open your heart and mind, like Kaito, and accept the rose and the thorns of life with equal respect and gratitude.

So, I invite you to take hold of your personal 'rose', with all its thorns and petals. Accept its entirety, and you'll see that inner peace is not far off.

Life is a tapestry of contrasts, and within those contrasts lies a deep and lasting peace.

The key to finding it is simply to accept, with love and mindfulnes, everything that life has to offer.

44.
The Full Moon:
The Wholeness of Inner Completion

That night, the starry sky seemed to have woven a silver mantle, and at the center of this magnificent celestial tapestry shone the full moon, a gem set in infinity. Hiroshi, the monk, left the monastery with a heartbeat of expectation, following an old moss-covered path that sinuously climbed towards a secluded hill. It was as if destiny itself was calling him.

Once he reached the top, he found an ancient boulder, smoothed by time and the elements, that seemed to have waited centuries for someone to understand its silent message. When he sat down, the boulder seemed to welcome him like an old friend. Hiroshi raised his eyes: the full moon looked at him, or so it seemed. He felt his heart expand, as if embracing a universal truth too vast to be expressed in words. In that moment, a wave of peace overwhelmed him, and Hiroshi knew he was complete. As if he had rediscovered a part of himself he thought was lost.

In the preceding weeks, Master Kaito had often spoken of inner completeness during the morning lessons. "Completeness," she explained, "is not something to be earned like a medal. It is a realization, a return to the source." But Hiroshi, like many others, had listened to these words as an unsolvable enigma, an ideal to perhaps reach one distant day.

At dawn, he returned to the monastery, his spirit laden with a tranquility never felt before. He found his master, Kaito, in the garden, among hibiscus and orchids, deep in reflection. "The full moon spoke to me," said Hiroshi, "not with words, but with a truth that permeated every fiber of my being. I felt completeness and knew I needed to seek no further."

Kaito looked up, and for a moment, Hiroshi saw something indescribable in her eyes – an infinite sea of understanding and love. "The moon has been a guide for many before you," said Kaito, "but few have truly listened. You have discovered that completeness is not a destination, but a state of being."

In the days and weeks to come, Hiroshi embodied that full moon for the other monks and for visitors seeking wisdom. Not because he had reached a goal, but because he had understood a fundamental truth: completeness is an internal journey, a recognition of what is already there.

Reflections

Have you ever gazed at the full moon in the night sky, seeking answers that always seem just out of reach?

In moments like these, how do you feel? Incomplete? In search of something you can't quite define?

Like Hiroshi, you may have sought answers in lessons, books, and dialogues. But have you ever considered that the completeness you desire is already inside you? Master Kaito states it clearly: completeness "is not something to be earned like a medal. It is a realization, a return to the source."

Have you ever taken a moment to reflect on this profound truth?

You might have lived your whole life searching for missing pieces. Maybe you've compared yourself to others, measuring your worth with scores, titles, or material possessions. But have you ever considered that the external search is a distraction from the internal journey you should be taking? The full moon in the story is not just an astronomical symbol; it is a reminder that completeness exists in a natural state, without the need for additions or alterations. What if the same is true for you?

When Hiroshi sits on the ancient boulder, he welcomes a moment of wordless truth, a moment that changes everything. And you? Are you willing to welcome those moments of silence in your life, to allow wisdom to emerge from the depths of your being? How often do you allow yourself to sit in silence, free your mind from distractions, and listen to the silent voice of your deeper self?

How often do you allow yourself to just be, without seeking, struggling, or yearning for something more?

Hiroshi becomes a full moon for others not because he has conquered a title or reached a milestone, but because he has understood a fundamental truth.

Completeness is not a destination but a recognition.

What if you, too, could become a full moon for others simply by embracing your essence, accepting yourself in all your magnificence and imperfection?

The story of Hiroshi invites us to explore a new path, one not marked by external milestones but by internal discoveries.

Remember, like the full moon in the night sky, you too have the capacity to feel complete at any moment.

Completeness is not a state to be achieved, but a reality to be recognized.

And once you recognize yourself as complete, you'll find that inner peace follows you like a friendly shadow at every step of your journey.

V
Conclusion

"The Eternal Flame"

Ignite Your Spirit
Live to the Fullest

The Eternal Flame:
Ignite Your Spirit and Live to the Fullest

"How do I feed my flame, Master?"

"First, be mindful. Mindfulness is like oxygen for the flame. If you are distracted or disconnected from yourself, how can your flame burn brightly?"

"Second, reflect. Self-reflection is the fuel. It's what allows your flame to grow, helping you understand yourself at ever-deeper levels."

"And the third?"

"Ah, the third is positive thinking. Imagine your flame dancing, filled with joy. This thought alone can bring you closer to the inner peace you seek."

"But remember, inner peace is a journey, not a destination. There's no end to the growth of your flame. Even when you believe you've reached a point of stability, there's always room for enlightenment."

So, I too invite you to nurture your inner flame.

Be mindful, reflect, and feed your spirit with positive thoughts. And in this way, your eternal flame will continue to grow, to shine, illuminating and warming not only you but all the fortunate ones around you.

Remember, inner peace is an endless journey. Start now and let your eternal flame burn endlessly.

Summary

If you have walked with me along this path of discoveries and enlightenment, you are now approaching the end of one phase and the beginning of a new one. Imagine each story told as a flame, much like the Zen candle in the temple of your soul. These individual and luminous flames have come together in a blazing bonfire, illuminating the path of your life.

"Ignite Your Spirit and Live to the Fullest," each flame is an invitation to keep the inner fire alive, never letting it extinguish.

I hope that these stories, like tiny mosaics, have composed a larger picture that has made you feel like you've acquired a treasure of wisdom – rich, multifaceted, and at times unexpected. Each lesson is like a North Star in the night, illuminating the path to a deeper understanding of yourself and the great mystery that is life.

On this mystical yet earthly journey, we have laughed and reflected, marveled and found keys – not to force rusty locks but to open doors that perhaps we didn't even know existed in the labyrinth of our consciousness. We sought treasures not in distant lands but in the fertile ground of our minds and hearts.

Just as a Zen master encourages you to see fullness in emptiness and simplicity in complexity, this book also aspires to be a silent friend rather than an authoritarian teacher. It doesn't aim to provide definitive answers but rather offers tools to formulate the right questions. Soul gardening is an endless art; it's not enough to sow once and wait for everything to grow on its own. Like a well-tended garden, it requires attention, love, and, above all, constant presence.

We explored the art of Mindfulness like a painter contemplates a canvas, adding color to gray moments and depth to bright ones. We ventured into the steep terrain of Self-Reflection, digging like archaeologists of our being to uncover forgotten artifacts of ourselves. With Positive Thinking, we learned to be captains of our destiny, not denying the presence of storms but navigating through them with strength and determination.

In the chapter on Inner Peace, we wove together the threads of these teachings into a tapestry that we hope can hang on the walls of your spirit, bringing with it lasting calm and tranquility. As the story of the "Eternal Flame" suggests, inner peace is not a place to reach but a light we carry with us, a beacon that illuminates both the unknown stretches of the journey and the familiar faces we encounter along the way.

Return to these stories whenever you feel like it, just as a pilgrim returns to a sanctuary that has touched their heart. Each visit offers a different revelation, a fresh interpretation. Like an oriental shadow theater, the lessons change depending on the light you project onto them.

This book is a station along the endless path of your life. It's not a final destination but a starting point. Every story, every thought, every single step is a seed planted in the garden of your future. So keep walking, keep sowing, and most importantly, keep living in this eternal present.

The road to inner peace can be as long as a lifetime and just as adventurous. But remember, with every step you take, you've already arrived. It's the act of walking itself that is the destination. Don't hesitate. Every step forward is a step toward yourself, a step toward inner peace. Every step is a new beginning.

Wait a moment.
Turn the page.
I want to express
to you my gratitude.

Acknowledgements

Dear Reader,

As we come to the end of this journey together, I first want to express my deepest gratitude to you.

Thank you for choosing to walk a part of this path with me, for sharing in the quest for serenity, and for allowing the Zen stories to kindle sparks of mindfulness in the quiet moments of your life. It is my sincere wish that the tales that have enriched my existence have been a source of inspiration and a guiding light for you.

Your voice and your experience are of immeasurable value to me.

If you feel inclined to share your thoughts, I would be grateful if you could take a moment to leave an honest review on the book's Amazon page. Your support is essential in helping me reach and inspire other readers in search of inner peace.

 Scan the QR code

to leave a review

With boundless gratitude and the hope that peace may always be your companion,

Sumitra Shakya

The Path to Inner Peace
Sumitra Shakya
sumitrashakyaauthor@gmail.com

The Path to Inner Peace
Sumitra Shakya
sumitrashakyaauthor@gmail.com

Impressum
The author is represented by
Giacomo Bruno
c/o IP-Management #21292
Ludwig-Erhard-Str. 18
20459 Hamburg, Germany